*Safe in His Sanctuary*

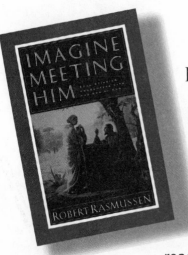

# ROBERT RASMUSSEN

*An Invitation*

*to the Wealth,*

*Warmth, and*

*Wonder of Christ*

# Safe
## IN HIS
# Sanctuary

Multnomah® Publishers *Sisters, Oregon*

SAFE IN HIS SANCTUARY

published by Multnomah Publishers, Inc.

and in association with Alive Communications
1465 Kelly Johnson Boulevard, Suite 320, Colorado Springs, Colorado 80920

© 1999 by Robert Rasmussen

*International Standard Book Number: 1-57673-408-0*

Cover photo of hands by Laura Benedict/Swanstock
Cover photo of tapestry by Lisa Taft Moore
Design by Kirk DouPonce

Printed in the United States of America

Unless otherwise indicated, Scripture quotations are from
*The Holy Bible,* New International Version (NIV) © 1973, 1984 by International
Bible Society used by permission of Zondervan Publishing House.
Also quoted: *The New American Standard Bible* (NASB)
©1960, 1977 by the Lockman Foundation.

*Multnomah* is a trademark of Multnomah Publishers, Inc.,
and is registered in the U.S. Patent and Trademark Office.
The colophon is a trademark of Multnomah Publishers, Inc.

For information:
MULTNOMAH PUBLISHERS, INC.•P.O. BOX 1720•SISTERS, OR 97759

Library of Congress Cataloging–in–Publication Data
Rasmussen, Robert, 1952–
Safe in His sanctuary/Robert Rasmussen. p.cm. Includes bibliographical references.
ISBN 1-57673-408-0 (alk. paper) 1. Christian life. 2. Jesus Christ—Mystical body. I. Title
BV4501.2.R327   1999   99-13513   CIP   248.4–dc21

99 00 01 02 03 04 05 06 — 10 9 8 7 6 5 4 3 2 1

To my wife, Lyn
From our two decades together
the insights in this book have come.

Michael Blackler put it well:
"There may be only one name on the cover
but there are definitely two lives inside."

Lyn, because of your greater sacrifice for the Savior,
I have learned to love Him, and you, more deeply.
And for that, I can't thank you enough.

# CONTENTS

## *First Hymn*

### THE UNTOLD STORY OF BETHLEHEM: *Our Wealth in the Son*

## *Second Hymn*

### THE HIDDEN HOPE OF GOLGOTHA: *Our Deliverance in the Son*

## *Third Hymn*

### THE UNCLUTTERED VIEW FROM OLIVET: *Our Safety in the Son*

# *Prayer*

## TO KNOW THE BEAUTY OF HIS SANCTUARY: *Our Quest for the Son*

# *Doxology*

## PRAISE FOR HIS TRAIL OF TRIUMPH: *Our Victory in the Son*

# Acknowledgments

This is just my second book. As I write the word *just,* I have to chuckle to myself because two books is one more than I thought I'd ever get a chance to write! Because I am so grateful for the unexpected blessing of penning this volume, I want to express my special thanks to Dan Benson (my efficient editor), Don Jacobson (the president with a personal touch), and all the others at Multnomah Publishers who decided to take a risk with a missionary in Africa. I cannot express to you how greatly you have blessed my life.

In form and approach, this book is quite different from the first. The vignette style of *Imagine Meeting Him* created a very unique book. But I knew that my second attempt needed to be different, lest I find myself in a rut. Being who I am, I wanted to share with my readers more about my own pilgrimage and struggles. I have done that in this book, and the process has been both scary and exhilarating. I offer it to you, my reader, feeling humbled by what I've revealed about myself but firm in my hope that you will identify with some part of my life and find healing for your own.

I have gained special encouragement in this process from some who have spoken or written uplifting words. They have been like those folks who help marathoners by handing them bottles of refreshing water. Thanks to Greg Gripentrog, Dick Hillis, Don and Nan Boesel, Diane Morris, and the whole crew at OC International for your support. To Dan Millheim for kind words. To Jack and Bonnie Rasmussen, Rich and Pam Rasmussen, and Scott and Diane Hefner—my siblings and their spouses, who have rejoiced with me and have been downright evangelistic about why all their friends need to go to the local bookstore. To Stan Jantz, Oscar Muriu, Vic Springer, Dan and Laurie King, the whole Perrin clan, and of course to Mom and Dad. Each has spurred me on.

God has given some of our friends a special calling. In the prime of life, they have been summoned to pain and suffering. They have been my models and inspiration as I have written about a place called Sanctuary. They are Michael and Sheila Blackler, Erik and Geneva Krag, Jeff, Kathy, and Joshua

Funk, and Paul and Mary Beckingham. You guys are my heroes.

How would we have come to understand adoption so deeply without the sovereign working of God through three special men? To Dad, who took up our cause. To Dr. Tom Perry, who heard our cry and became a special friend. And to Doug Schultz, longtime buddy turned attorney, who got us through the legal hoops. I owe chapter 3 to you three.

I want to thank Dr. Ed Murphy for showing me that Ephesians 1 ought to be the bread and butter of every Christian. Your teaching on spiritual warfare during OC internship changed my life and became the driving passion of this book.

Thank you again, Kathy Yanni of Alive Communications, for helping me at those critical decision points. Your counsel always has the ring of wisdom about it, and I appreciate your sensitivity to the Spirit of God, not just to "the biz." And to Greg Johnson, also of Alive Communications, for opening that first packet and thinking it deserved a second look. Thanks, too, to Lisa Lauffer who has made the editing phase a breeze.

And finally to my two daughters, Lauren and Heather. You've made your dad and mom proud. Thanks for letting me share your stories with others and for being patient when you needed to use the computer.

BOB RASMUSSEN
Nairobi, Kenya

# The Sanctuary

ave you ever been at risk? Ever felt in danger? I don't mean the desirable kind of risk we occasionally feel the need to take, such as launching a new business venture or getting married. Nor do I refer to the bungee-jumping kind of risk that some seek for the thrill of it.

I mean the bone-chilling, threatening situations we'd all like to avoid.

I have an early recollection of facing such danger. I was a young boy crossing a busy boulevard on my own. I very carefully watched all four lanes (two in each direction) for oncoming cars. Seeing that the first two lanes were clear, I walked in the crosswalk until I made it safely to the median. I had just two more lanes to go. The traffic was heavy, but I was prepared to wait until I could safely cross the rest of the street. Unexpectedly, I got a lucky break. The driver in the lane closest to me noticed my plight and stopped to let me cross. I began to skip happily, and obliviously, across both lanes, only to realize almost too late that another car was rapidly approaching in the other lane. It barely missed me.

Danger. Fear. What are your memories of such risk? Maybe you endured a house fire or a burglary. Perhaps you nearly drowned or injured yourself in a fall. Maybe you've experienced a life-threatening illness. These and many other situations can paralyze us with fear.

Now let's switch gears. Think of a time when you felt totally safe (I hope you have such a recollection). Let me tell you, once I made it unharmed across that final lane (with my heart thumping in my throat), I felt safe! What do you recall? Fishing beside a calm river on a warm day? Looking through boxes of memories in the attic with your mother? Being rescued from a sinking canoe or being enfolded in your father's arms after walking home in the dark?

One of our strongest emotions is fear, and one of our greatest yearnings is for safety. This truth has not escaped God's notice. Just as any loving father has a strong instinct to protect and provide for his children, so our heavenly Father cannot bear for His children to feel afraid. He loves to come to the rescue, delights in pulling our sinking boat to shore and feeding us by the fire. God desires to provide hope to the wife who feels abandoned in her marriage, wisdom to the parent who is losing a child to wrong influences. Our Father sees us when we're discouraged or lonely, and He wants to reach out with a helping hand. He knows when we're caught in the quagmire of sin, and He yearns to throw us a rope.

For these and a thousand other reasons, our loving Father has prepared a refuge for His children. A place where we fugitives can find safe haven, where we refugees can enjoy shelter from our pursuers. A place where the tired, the hungry, the desperate can find an oasis in the desert. Where the stressed and harried can regain peace of mind. This place the Father has prepared offers asylum for those who feel misunderstood and falsely accused. It offers protection for those tormented by demons of lust and hate. It provides love, care, and comfort for those who feel lonely and abandoned.

Who wouldn't want to be in such a Sanctuary? Who among us doesn't quietly cry out for such a safe haven?

We need not cry out for it any longer. We need no longer yearn for such safe refuge. For such a place exists, not just for us to visit for a time but for us to inhabit. And in this book, we'll explore this Sanctuary that God has created just for us; we'll examine its details and experience the sensations of being happy and undisturbed within it.

How can we do this in a book? Don't we need to travel to some ornate, glorious structure somewhere far away? Not at all. You see, the Sanctuary of which I speak is not one with pillars and archways that an architect would design. It's not crafted by stone masons or metalworkers. Instead, this Sanctuary is a *spiritual* safe house God has created for us to enjoy forever.

But how can we of finite understanding learn about things so far beyond us? How can people of flesh and blood discover such glorious things?

*A*s we explore this Sanctuary, two sources will guide us. The first source for our exploration comes from the first chapter of Ephesians. When its author, the apostle Paul, sat in Rome under house arrest, God gave Paul not just a glimpse but a real taste of the Sanctuary. The Spirit who inspired Paul to write this epistle gave him a clear and undistorted view of life in that sacred place and did so with the intention that we should enter in and experience it by faith.

The second source for our exploration will be the Gospel accounts of Jesus Christ's life and ministry. These ancient records describe the time when the kingdom of God came near, a time during which humankind took a glimpse into the Sanctuary. Because, you see, the Sanctuary isn't a place; it's a *person.* Jesus Christ is our place of refuge. And though humankind in Jesus' day may not have seen all that Christ had to offer them, we can now delve into the written records of that era and take a second, longer look into the Sanctuary.

These two sources won't merely guide us on a *tour* of the Sanctuary. A tour informs and illustrates but leaves one feeling detached from what he or she sees. God isn't interested in having tourists in the Sanctuary. He wants participants and dwellers.

So God, through the inspired writings of Ephesians 1, brings us right into the experience of the Sanctuary, into a grand worship service! God's Spirit has written the music; all believers sing and play it. And throughout this book, we will partake in this worship of our Lord.

We will sing the lyrics of three masterful hymns that tell of the Sanctuary of Jesus and of what God did to bring us there. As we sing the first hymn, "The Untold Story of Bethlehem," we will learn of the incredible blessings God has granted us in Jesus Christ as an outgrowth of God's eternal love for us and His commitment to gather for Himself a holy family.

Our worship will then proceed to "The Hidden Hope of Golgotha," a hymn that begins with the sobering reality of our unworthiness and inability to enter the Sanctuary by ourselves. As the hymn continues, the lyrics chronicle the glorious work Christ has done to deliver us from our deadly fate by qualifying us completely for entrance into that divine refuge.

The final hymn provides the perfect climax to that which has gone before.

"The Uncluttered View from Olivet" expounds our rightful confidence that the Holy Spirit has guaranteed forever our life in the Sanctuary.

In response to the truths these hymns express, the apostle Paul, sitting in a Roman detention house yet at the same time dwelling in the Sanctuary, offers up a prayer: "To Know the Beauty of His Sanctuary." It is the prayer of one who has experienced life in Christ. In recording this prayer for us, Paul teaches us how to pray in the Sanctuary. This prayer leads us away from our mundane repetition and takes us instead into the realm of adoration of our Master.

No wonder such prayer leads us to a doxology to our conquering Savior. "Praise for His Trail of Triumph" brings us to the summit of our Sanctuary experience by reminding us that we have experienced the victory of Christ's resurrection and ascension into heaven.

So come. Come with your baggage. Bring all your fears. That's right, pack your inadequacies and self-doubts. Depression? Boredom? Throw them all into your bag and bring them along. For the Father has designed this haven specifically for folks such as us.

I don't know you personally, but I know you've been through a lot. I know you've struggled. How do I know this? Because we all have. Still are. We're battered. Some of us are bruised more than others, but we all need refuge. So I invite you to the oasis in the desert, the shelter in the storm. I invite you into life in Christ. Come, be safe in His Sanctuary.

# First

# Hymn

# The Untold Story of Bethlehem
## Our Wealth in the Son

*Praise be to the God and Father of our Lord Jesus Christ,*

*who has blessed us in the heavenly realms*

*with every spiritual blessing in Christ.*

*For he chose us in him before the creation of the world*

*to be holy and blameless in his sight.*

*In love he predestined us to be adopted as his sons through Jesus Christ,*

*in accordance with his pleasure and will—*

*to the praise of his glorious grace,*

*which he has freely given us in the One he loves.*

EPHESIANS 1:3–6

*How little we knew that when Jesus was born*

*the Father had already enfolded us in His love*

*from forever past.*

*D*o you remember those early childhood years when the worst tragedy imaginable was your mother calling you in for dinner? Those were the days. You had shoes for your feet, food for your stomach, and friends for your heart. You were rich! No playground bullies yet. No homework. No alphabet to master. No phonics to decipher. Just life as it was meant to be.

For the preschooler.

But alas, time marched on like a gruff sergeant. Responsibilities ensued. No longer could you sleep as long as you wanted to. No, you had to be up and out of bed in order to please the unbending master that has hounded you ever since: the schedule.

Bit by bit, childhood freedom surrendered to adulthood obligation. Where you used to live for yourself and whatever fun you could find, you discovered a tough master called a teacher. And she was only the first in line, for in the years to come supervisors and officials, coaches and creditors followed. Even spouses and children fell in line to make their demands.

Before you knew it, life in the sandbox had sifted through your miniature fingers, and now you find yourself in unfriendly places where you're valued only if you perform. You had inadequate time to rehearse. The demands have been rigorous. And perhaps you now find yourself at a standstill, in a dead-end job or a stalemate marriage.

Life can be hazardous.

Fortunately, someone watches this oppressive process with a keen eye of interest. God notices the increasing burden on your back. He sees the strain. And He says, "May I restore those carefree years? Would you allow me to return to you the security you felt before life became treacherous?"

You're probably wondering where He said that. Well, He didn't exactly say it in so many words, but He has shown it in so many, many ways. The story of God's restoring our safety began in that special manger we recall annually. I'm not talking just now about the details of the shepherds and sheep, the star, or the angelic choir. I'm referring to the divine backdrop to the nativity crèche. Why did God the Father send Jesus to earth? Why did God the Son agree to come? Why did God the Holy Spirit oversee every detail? Here's why: *at the*

*Incarnation, God gladly took a risk to give us safety.* He went out on a limb so that we could come in from the cold.

If that's not a love story, I've never heard one.

*B*y giving us Jesus, God gave us a safe haven, a place where no one can harm us or steal us away. He gave us a Sanctuary, offering us full protection under the eternal law of the divine Advocate. He gave a place of untold wealth to us who will leave this life as starkly naked as we entered it.

You don't have to look very far in Scripture to pick up the thread of this love story. It's everywhere. But at certain points God lays it out nice and plain, giving us a clear vision of the Sanctuary.

Of all those places, none is more awesome than the opening of Paul's letter to the Ephesians. There, God pulls back the veil and bids us enter the Sanctuary. There He allows us to taste life in Christ. And when we do, we find ourselves in the middle of a worship experience. The lyrics are hymnlike. The praise is Him-like.

The curtain is open. The invitation stands. They're worshiping inside. Let's go in. You'll have shoes for your feet, food for your stomach, and friends for your heart. Happy days are here again!

# Refugees Like Us

*God has created a wonderful place where*
*earthlings can receive the treasure chest of heaven.*

My friend Keith Brown had a group of us howling one morning over his true-life story about some friends and a jeep.

It happened in the Philippines, where Keith served as a missionary. Some friends were visiting from the United States, and Keith took them into the country in a kind of passenger jeep called a *jeepney*. (A jeepney, which has open sides, is the kind of vehicle invented for humid countries where you sweat more than you shiver.) The visitors were hanging out the sides, enjoying the view of the lush countryside. Some of them may have been smiling.

The detail about smiling may seem unimportant now, but that's because I haven't yet mentioned the water buffalo. Or, to be more precise, about what the water buffalo had left in the middle of the road.

Apparently this particular water buffalo had enjoyed a huge dinner followed by a big country breakfast. Nature's inevitable call must have beckoned him around 9:00 A.M., right to the middle of that country road. I include this unpleasant thought only because you need to know that as Keith's jeep approached it, the buffalo pile was huge, fresh, and steaming in the sunlight.

Have you ever witnessed an unfolding disaster, powerless to stop it? Well, the American visitors weren't the only ones driving that country road at 9:15 A.M. that day. A huge lorry (that's what most of the world calls a truck) full of goods was lumbering along as well. Maybe the driver was tired, or maybe he was just a lousy driver. Or perhaps he had a mischievous streak. Whatever the case, as the lorry and the jeep approached each other, the lorry driver hit that buffalo pile at full gale and blasted a spray of farm-fresh fertilizer right into those smiling American faces.

Please don't consider me crass (either for telling that story or for asking you this question), but has the lorry of life ever delivered you an unwanted load of the dregs? Ever received a faceful of the worst you could imagine?

Timing isn't everything, but it's awfully close. Being in the wrong place at the wrong time can wilt even the bravest smile.

This idea reminds me of another one of my friends. He calls himself Ishimwe. He prefers not to use his real name. As I said, timing is everything, and Ishimwe knows this firsthand. You see, Ishimwe was living in his homeland, Rwanda, when it became a powder keg. When Rwanda blew up, Ishimwe was on the wrong side of the fence and had to leave. The lorry got there first and plastered him.

And that's how I met him. Ishimwe came to Kenya, my current home, using his made-up name. He still has parents in his home country, and a fiancée too. In other words, his body isn't where his heart is. Maybe Ishimwe illustrates an apt definition for *refugee* that the United Nations would like to borrow sometime: folks who left home for all the wrong reasons.

Refugees are everywhere. Both kinds. There are refugees such as Ishimwe, people on the move. Like nomads, they constantly pull up tent pegs in search of a fresh water hole. But unlike nomads, most refugees aren't out in the desert. They're right under our noses, in our towns, in our big cities. I see them in Nairobi every day. They seek refuge in the anonymity of the masses. And it works. This type of refugee is faceless. She may be that unkempt woman carrying an unwashed child. He may be that businessman with the leather briefcase. They are forms in a crowd. Solitary, unheard cries in a cacophany of pain. Anonymous waves in a sea of need.

Then there are *refugees like us*. How often have we hidden in the masses, hurting in secret? How often have we yearned for refreshment in our desert, longing for a place to call home?

We have a refugee problem in the church, and we're a part of it. Too many of us live barren and pointless lives, even as Christians. Reluctant nomads with-out tents, we're on the run emotionally, searching for a relationship that satis-fies. Harrassed and unsettled, contentment eludes us like a mirage. Our daily terrain is dry and silent. We inch through our days, parched and hopeless.

For that reason, God has placed within easy reach a tropical oasis where the water is sweet and the air is cool. It's a Sanctuary for the harried. It's safety for refugees like us. Listen to the activity inside. I like to think of it as a worship service. "Blessed be the God and Father of our Lord Jesus Christ, who has blessed us with every spiritual blessing" (Ephesians 1:3, NASB).

Perhaps more than anything else, we who wander like nomads at heart desire to be blessed. We need to be loved and appreciated, even wanted and needed. Yet few people go out of their way to bless refugees. Most people ignore them, pretending they don't exist.

But God isn't like most people. He seeks to bless us refugees with *every spiri-tual blessing*. And aren't we glad?

## No Leftovers, Please

With this oasis in the desert, the promise of every spiritual blessing, Paul begins the first hymn we sing in the Sanctuary. And, uncharacteristically, he does so with great passion. Usually Paul exhibits logical thinking, laying down coherent arguments that lead readers from one point to the next. Or he introduces his comments with a personal note to the church or a reference to some local issue, and expounds on them.

But when Paul begins Ephesians, his spirit seems so full of emotional praise that he literally explodes from the starting gate with adoration of God.[1] I can imagine Paul, under Roman house arrest with the guard not far away, calling for his scribe and demanding, "Write!" His assistant fumbles for his quill pen and papyrus and finally says, "Ready." Then Paul unleashes that which he can no longer restrain:

**Blessed** *be the God and Father of our Lord Jesus Christ, who has* **blessed** *us with every spiritual* **blessing.**

You see, if the apostle had had the presence of mind to explain everything logically, he would have begun with what is now Ephesians 2:1, "As for you, you were dead in your transgressions and sins," describing the spiritual bankruptcy that necessitates the Sanctuary. But in this instance, Paul doesn't write primarily from his mind. Instead, he's on fire in his spirit! His heart is ignited with passion for the God who blesses us.[2] And thanks to Paul's willingness to set aside logic in deference to the Holy Spirit's leading, we now enjoy the first chapter of Ephesians. We've received the hymns of the Sanctuary!

And the first hymn is all about blessing. "God is to be blessed," says the singing. "Why?" we ask. "Because God has blessed us," says the song. "And how has he blessed us?" we might wonder. "He has blessed us with every spiritual blessing." Oh, sing it: *every spiritual blessing!*

Not a few odds and ends of blessing. But *every* blessing. God has love and grace and forgiveness to give us. His storehouse contains encouragement for the depressed, deliverance for the tempted, comfort for the grieved, protection for the oppressed.

You would never overhear God muttering to Himself, "Now where was that other blessing? I thought I had that one, but maybe I got confused and actually never did." No, God legitimately possesses every spiritual blessing. Otherwise He couldn't rightfully give them away.

No wonder Paul was so passionate! He had meditated on God's blessings, remembering God's vast wealth of them. He considered God's spiritual treasure chest containing adoption and redemption and forgiveness and grace and wisdom and understanding and mystery and truth and gospel and sealing and inheritance...all the eternal treasures that God longs to give away!

But how could Paul understand the meanings of these blessings so well? Probably because he got a glimpse of them. Remember that Paul describes (in 2 Corinthians 12:1–4) a weird experience he had. (I call it weird because Paul himself didn't know exactly what it was and whether he was "in the body" when it happened.) In this experience God brought Paul to the <u>third heaven</u> and gave him a peek into the treasure chest of blessings.

I emphasize this matter because of where the blessings are located: "in the heavenly realms with every spiritual blessing in Christ." The heavenly realms!

Can you fathom that? Heaven, where we will finally experience true reality. Heaven, where resides everything permanent, lasting, and significant. Heaven, which bursts at the seams with the riches God wants to give us!

But if the blessings are in heaven, how will God deliver them to us on earth? After all, "there are also heavenly bodies and there are earthly bodies; but the splendor of the heavenly bodies is one kind, and the splendor of the earthly bodies is another" (1 Corinthians 15:40). The problem is as real as the treasures: the gifts are of the gold dust of heaven, but the receivers are of the humble dust of the earth. How can the eternal and heavenly be delivered meaningfully and understandably to those who are temporal and earthly?

And from our perspective, how can we, so limited and small and blind, find our way to the blessings of heaven? Could we meditate with so much concentration as to visualize our heavenly and hoped-for inheritance? Could we be moral enough to impress God and merit a tidbit or two of His kindness? Could we offer up our bodies in martyrdom for some worthy, even religious, cause?

No. Even if we excelled in these activities, we'd end up empty-handed.

The God of the blessings wants to *give* them away, and He has created a wonderful place where earthlings can receive the treasure chest of heaven. Despite our best efforts, we could hardly build a place that adequately expresses God's eternal love. Nor could we construct a venue to safely display every spiritual blessing. Only God could conceive of a Sanctuary like that.

And only God could make it possible for us to enter in. Surely the convergence of God's love, God's blessings, and God's beloved ones is the miracle of the ages...

## A.D. 51, Corinth, in the Artisan's Quarter

*"A record of the genealogy of Jesus Christ*
*the son of David,*
*the son of Abraham..."*

Paul read the words aloud, savoring their familiarity. He had recently acquired a portion of Matthew's Gospel and planned to expound on it in the synagogue next Sabbath.

*"Abraham was the father of Isaac,*
*Isaac the father of Jacob,*
*Jacob the father of Judah and his brothers…"*

Nearby, Aquila and his wife Priscilla were finishing the last of the stitching on a tent, a special order for an upcoming wedding.

"Of all the tents we make, I always love stitching together a new home for a bride and groom," Priscilla mused, loud enough for the two men to hear. "It's wonderful to think of the intimacy and fun the couple will share within this tent."

"No kidding," quipped her husband with a chuckle. "And before long the gurgling sounds of a little one will be heard as well."

At this point their mentor entered the conversation. "Do you all remember the tentmakers' life verse? 'The Lord has been our dwelling place in all generations.'"

"Written, I believe, by one who dwelt in tents: Moses," added Aquila. "I've always been fascinated with the tent of meeting that Moses set up outside the people's camp. Wouldn't it have been wonderful to seek the Lord there?"

"A tradition," Paul continued, "that led to the Tabernacle. I must preach sometime on that verse from Exodus where God said, 'Then have them make a sanctuary for me, and I will dwell among them.'"

Priscilla brought the conversation back to the matter at hand. "Someone had to make Moses' tent, and tentmakers put together the Tabernacle, I believe. And I know a wedding couple who needs shelter tomorrow night!"

Aquila resumed his stitching, Paul his reading:

*"Salmon the father of Boaz,*
*    whose mother was Rahab,*
*Boaz the father of Obed,*
*    whose mother was Ruth,*
*Obed the father of Jesse,*
*    and Jesse the father of King David…"*

He paused for reflection, which didn't last long.

"I couldn't help but notice the presence of Rahab and Ruth in our Lord's genealogy," Priscilla observed as she punched her needle through the goatskin.

"We could hardly overemphasize the importance of women," agreed her husband, wizened by many years of marriage. "But Jesse's name caught my attention. What is that passage in Isaiah, Paul—the one about the branch? Do you know that one from memory?"

The apostle quoted it:

*"A shoot will come up from the stump of Jesse;*
*from his roots a Branch will bear fruit.*
*The Spirit of the LORD will rest on him—*
*the Spirit of wisdom and of understanding,*
*the Spirit of counsel and of power,*
*the Spirit of knowledge and of the fear of the LORD."*

Priscilla and Aquila reflected as they sealed off the last seam and began to gather the leather scraps from the ground. They discussed briefly the custom of putting gifts in the newlyweds' wedding tent. They wondered if this particular tent would be blessed

with nard
　　or frankincense,
　　　　with myrrh
　　　　　　or even with gold.

Paul reached the end of the genealogy, reading the climax with increasing volume and gusto meant for the neighboring artisans to hear:

*"Eliud the father of Eleazar,*
*Eleazar the father of Matthan,*
*Matthan the father of Jacob,*
*and Jacob the father of Joseph,*
*the husband of Mary, of whom was born Jesus,*
*who is called Christ."*

Priscilla again noted the feminine aspect of the list. She wished she could have been in Israel at that time. She wondered what Mary knew of the baby she bore. She recalled Mary's praise: "My soul glorifies the Lord and my spirit rejoices in God my Savior."

Like Mary, she sat for a while and pondered these things in her heart.

The tent was ready for the new family.[3]

## The Tent is Fully Stocked

Fellow refugees, there's only one place God could create where we could experience His love and receive His blessings. God has conceived of that place and has prepared it carefully: "The Word became flesh and made his dwelling among us. We have seen his glory, the glory of the One and Only, who came from the Father, full of grace and truth" (John 1:14). The unique place God has prepared is none other than the eternal Word, the Son of God, who pitched His tent among us and became our Sanctuary.[4]

We're homeless no more. No need to run and hide any longer. God has made it possible for us to dwell in Christ and receive His bountiful gifts and blessings.

And He desires that we feel secure in our relationship with Him, no longer basing our acceptance on the cracked foundation of our performance but on the sure slab of His unfailing commitment to us. God aims to crash the notion that His children must live in a state of spiritual hand-to-mouth. He has made us rich in Christ. As we dwell and worship in the Sanctuary, we'll find the "Jesus tent" stocked full with priceless gifts...

every spiritual blessing in Christ
　　chosen in Christ
　　　　adopted through Jesus Christ
　　　　　　given grace freely in the one He loves
　　　　　　　　redeemed in Him
　　　　　　　　　　purposed in Christ
　　　　　　　　　　　　all things summed up in Christ
　　　　　　　　　　　　　　included in Christ
　　　　　　　　　　　　　　　　marked in Him with a seal.

When God gave His Son as our Savior, He committed Himself to giving a complete treasure chest of blessings. The Father so designed the blessings that anyone who received *one* of them would receive *all* of them. It would be as impossible to receive half of the blessings as it would be to receive half of God's Son, for the treasure comes as a package called *Jesus*.

How could God care so much about our condition? How could He give such attention to the details of our need? Is the answer not found in His loving character? Can we not depend on Him to always show love toward us? The fact is, God can't help but be generous.

Two boys walked down a street in their neighborhood. They were raising money for a school project by selling candy to their neighbors.

At least they were *trying* to sell candy. They weren't having much luck.

As they approached the biggest house on the street, one boy, the more experienced of the two, said to the other, "The man at this next house will buy some candy from us."

His younger companion was skeptical, even contrary. He argued that rich people just don't bother.

But the more experienced one maintained his confidence, repeating that the man in the big house would buy.

So the boys went up to the door and knocked on it. The owner of the house came to the door personally. He didn't need to ask what the boys wanted, for he could easily see they were selling candy. He smiled. He said he would like to buy some candy today. And he did.

The door closed gently behind the boys, and they walked along the pathway together. The skeptical boy was stunned. "How did you know that he was going to buy some candy?"

The other boy answered, savoring the moment. "I've sold candy on this street many times before," he said. "And there's one thing I've learned about that man. He always buys!"[5]

God wants to change your image of Him. He wants you to know that He's rich and that He has deposited untold wealth for you in Christ. Isn't it about time we started taking God at His word?

*I*'ve noted one thing about many refugees, especially those who have never known any other way to live. They're so accustomed to roughing it that they can't relax when circumstances improve. They become so used to eking out an existence that they can't enjoy wealth should it befall them. If someone grants them safe haven, they're suspicious, waiting for the inevitable turn for the worse.

Sorry for getting personal, but don't you think we ought to give God another chance?

*Forgive me Lord, for often forgetting*

*or even doubting Your love for me.*

*Forgive me for thinking that I don't have very much*

*when in fact I have everything in Christ.*

*And forgive me for seeing so much duty*

*in my walk with You.*

*Why do I so often see You as someone trying to get rather than someone*

*who has been giving all along?*

*Thank You, Jesus,*

*for pitching Your tent among us and asking us*

*to come inside with You.*

*Thank You, Father,*

*for stocking the tent with so many gifts.*

*O angels, keep praising Him!*

*Glory to God in the highest,*

*and on earth peace to men on whom His favor rests.*

*And let us join them, O Church.*

*Praise be to the God and Father of our Lord Jesus Christ, who has*

*blessed us in the heavenly realms*

*with every spiritual blessing in Christ!*

**WARNING TO THE READER:**

The following chapter contains mature subject matter. In fact, you've probably learned to fear, or maybe just ignore, some of the concepts we'll discuss. But as touchy as it may be to do so, we must deal with these subjects fearlessly. Let me tell you why. Though too high to completely grasp, these concepts are also too wonderful to be ignored. They are two precious jewels in God's treasure chest of blessings, two of the most intimate love words in God's vocabulary. The concepts of which I speak? Election and predestination. Proceed, not with caution, but with joyful expectation!

# *The Rightful Owner*

*The Sanctuary isn't the place where God decided to gather holy people.
It is where He chose to gather people to make them holy.*

**I**t's interesting what we remember from childhood. Usually it's a crisis event or an exciting experience that lodges itself deeply enough in one's subconscious mind that it stands the test of time and lingers in memory for years.

One of my unforgettable experiences involves an awards ceremony I attended as a seven-year-old boy. It sticks in my mind not because of the fame it brought to my little world but because of an inner battle it forced me to fight.

During this awards ceremony, no words could have shocked me more than two words, "Bobby Rasmussen," the name of my youth. Upon hearing these words, I was supposed to rise from my seat, walk to the front of the room, and receive a ribbon for winning a running race. Numbly, I did so. I felt the whole world watching me, and I wanted to transform myself into a piece of dust, climb under a carpet, and hide—anything to get out of that suffocating room.

You see, I had no recollection of winning that race.

Having collected the ribbon, I returned to my seat and slumped into it, my conscience stricken. I looked down at the ribbon in my hand. Who did this really belong to? I felt so bad about the mistake that I wanted to just ditch the award.

But not completely. I had an inner conflict going on. The ribbon was very pretty. I could envision it pinned to the wall in our house, drawing admiration from all who gazed at it. And, after all, maybe I had won that race.

The awards ceremony ended, and everyone but me was talking and having a good time. I, on the other hand, was miserable. I was sweating with panic. What should I do? I couldn't bear the insecurity and guilt mingled with the wishful longing. I just knew the leader would figure out the mistake, return to the microphone, and say, "Ladies and gentlemen, before you leave, I have to make one correction: Bobby Rasmussen *did not* win that race and therefore *should not* have received that pretty ribbon I gave him. Will Bobby please advance to the podium immediately and *give it back?*"

And since you too were once seven years old, you know that that would have killed me! The very threat of it happening was excruciating.

Contrary to my fears, no such announcement took place. But I sat by myself, feeling sick to my stomach, ensnared by the agony of my conscience.

This inner struggle of a young boy mirrors the very battle that so many believers face. We read in the Bible that God has awarded us the first-place ribbon His Son won for us, but we live life feeling as if we received it by mistake. We fear that God will clear His throat at the microphone of eternity and say, "Attention, everyone. In reviewing our records, it has come to My attention that a number of blessings have been given out by mistake. We are sorry for this awkward situation, but I must ask that those who have received their blessings in error—you know who you are—please come to the throne and return the blessings to their rightful owners. Thank you."

Their "rightful owners." Do you feel the longing in those words? Oh, to rightfully own that which you prize! Nothing to fear. Hiding no secrets. Dreading no last-minute announcements.

After the awards ceremony broke up, I mustered the courage to seek out the award-giver. I don't remember if that person was a man or woman, tall or short. I only know that I needed one small bit of information from him or her. (Amazing how insecurity can destroy a seven-year-old or, for that matter, a seventy-seven-year-old.) I had to know if that award truly belonged to me.

With a distinct vibrato caused by the shaking of my little legs, I approached this person and asked my simple question. "Did I...really win this award? Is this really...mine?" *Well, now I've done it. I've gone and opened my big mouth and ruined everything. I could have had this ribbon in my room at home, but no, I had to mess it up. Now I'll have to give it back.*

"Of course that's your ribbon, Bobby."

In six words, the award-giver had changed my little world. He had solved my massive dilemma. His words of authority removed my pumped-up fears and insecurities. How? He told me I was the rightful owner of the prize.

Now I could enjoy it! I ran to my parents and displayed my ribbon proudly. I had held it before, but now I owned it! My conscience was relieved. My guilt had vanished. I was safe and secure in the knowledge that what I would hang on my wall really belonged there.

Welcome to the Sanctuary.

Welcome to the place where the blessings truly belong to you.

Walk up to that throne and ask your question: "Lord, are all these blessings really mine? Did You truly mean to give them to me?"

And let the relief and excitement shiver from your spine all the way down to your toes. "Yes, dear one. Jesus ran the race on your behalf. The prize is rightfully yours!"

Fears, insecurities, guilt, and doubt, be gone!

## Because God Chose

Diseases plague our world. Malaria, cholera, and typhoid are wiping out scores of families. But let me tell you about a largely unpublicized epidemic: the widespread blight of spiritual insecurity.

Believers by the thousands are passing in and out of churches, unaware that they rightfully own every spiritual blessing in Christ. They doubt themselves, chide themselves, and even hate themselves.

One reason so many of us lack confidence in our standing before God is that we have the wrong view of the Sanctuary, our life in Jesus. Specifically, we have the wrong view of the door that leads to the Sanctuary. We picture that door as having a handle, but we mentally place the handle on the wrong side. We think it belongs on our side, making it our responsibility to open the door and enter in. And if this is the case, then perhaps it's our job to *keep* ourselves inside as well.

But the fact is, the handle is on God's side. He opens the door.

VISION: WELS UN DOOR TU MY
HEART

Pick up the melody of the Sanctuary hymn. Locate the door handle properly as you sing along:

> Who has blessed us in the heavenly realms with every spiritual blessing
> in Christ. For he chose us in him before the creation of the world to
> be holy and blameless in his sight. (Ephesians 1:3–4)

"He chose us." Now I realize this is a difficult doctrine, even a controversial one. But let's not allow controversy to rob the church of its joy, of *our* joy. He chose us!

Come back to Bethlehem's manger with me for a moment and consider: Why Mary? Is it important that it wasn't Esther, the herbalist's daughter, or Rachel, that nice young girl engaged to the new priest? Or what about Naomi, the women's leader with a real heart for God? Of all women, why Mary?

I can't wait to meet her, the mother of Jesus. The donkey-riding, secret-keeping teenager who, perhaps while washing dishes one evening, turned around to put a plate in the cabinet and saw a six-foot-five-inch angel named Gabriel. What went through her mind at that instant? That's what I want to ask her. And what incredible thoughts jammed her brain when a booming voice proceeded from this man she had never invited into her kitchen, saying, "Greetings, you who are highly favored! The Lord is with you" (Luke 1:28).

Did Mary possess a special personality trait that God wanted to incorporate into His incarnate Son's genetic makeup? Was she the holiest woman in the history of the world and therefore the likeliest, most deserving candidate?

Funny, you'd think that if such were the case the Scriptures would communicate that fact to us. But the biblical account leads us to believe that merit did not win Mary the honor of birthing the Savior. She didn't win first place in some "Mother of the Savior" contest.

God chose Mary for a reason, and He wasn't secretive about it. In fact, He instructed Gabriel to make it plain: Mary, he said, you are "highly favored."

Which has me repeating myself: Why Mary?

Because God looked over all the women of all history and did something very Godlike.

He chose.

He favored Mary. He didn't pay her for something she had earned, didn't reimburse her with what she had coming to her. By grace, He decided to favor her.

Same subject, different scene. God didn't create the Sanctuary for His own entertainment. It wasn't an experiment in cosmic sociology. No, God created the Sanctuary as a place to pour out His goodness on a group of people. But why you? Why me?

Because God looked out and saw men and women, boys and girls, who were putting plates in cabinets, driving to job sites, tending crops, or going to school, and time after time He did something very Godlike.

He chose.

You. And me.

To *choose* means to "call out," not in the sense of getting our attention but in the sense of calling us out from the rest to belong to Him, to dwell in the Sanctuary.

How do you react to that? I sometimes wonder how Mary reacted to God's favoring her, if she searched her own mind for reasons He chose her. "Was it something I did that pleased God?" If she reasoned along those lines, I'd guess she also had some troubling doubts such as "Has God missed some of the things I've done that should disqualify me?" For her sake, I hope Mary eventually concluded that God chose her not because of any merit of her own but simply because He wanted to.

God chose her because He chose her. Period.

There's nothing more reassuring than the raw sovereignty of God.

Now, if you're a member of the same human race I belong to, then you, like the rest of us, may often doubt your worthiness for blessing. You occasionally think that things are going well for you only because God has overlooked something, and that when He discovers the missing piece, the good will melt away into the awfulness you deserve.

But I ask you to tune in to the worship of the Sanctuary and let the first hymn's words wash over your doubting mind. He chose us. He chose you. Why? Because He did something very Godlike. He chose to.

## The Gall of God

Conventional wisdom says that God's choosing is a bogus idea. "God should not have been selective. Instead He should have insisted that everyone be saved."

Oh, should He? Should God have coerced people against their will to accept His offer? Should He have created a family that included squirming rebels who prefer darkness to His light?

"All right, then, He should have delegated the choosing to us so we could give passes to the Sanctuary democratically. That way it wouldn't be so lopsided with some peoples of the world having many believers and others so few."

Really? How impartial and objective would we be when the stakes are eternal life? How readily would we choose someone from a different ethnic group or country at the expense of denying the right to someone in our own town or family? Humankind has shown no such skill at being unbiased.

"Well, then, God should have made it completely voluntary. Whoever wanted to enter could do so. That way, no one wanting entrance into the Sanctuary would be left out."

That's an interesting protest and hard to argue with. In fact, we need to say that God chose those who could enter *and* He also made entrance voluntary. (Seems contradictory, doesn't it?) Do you know anyone who is being excluded against his or her will? If people haven't entered the Sanctuary, it's because they have chosen not to. Or they haven't heard that they can, in which case God's choosing them is their only hope.

And so, in spite of the objections of conventional human wisdom, God proceeds according to His plan. And He has the gall to do so without apology or excuse. The only explanation offered is that He chose us "in Him."

Somehow, Jesus is the only explanation of election. Long ago, before the crossbars of governments were lifted into place, before the pillars of society were raised, even before the foundation of the world was laid, God the Father looked at His Son with loving eyes and envisioned for Him a committed people.

He pictured His Son as the King of kings and knew who would be His loyal subjects.

He considered Jesus as a groom and He chose for Him an appropriate bride.

He thought of His Son as the head of the Church, and it apparently came into clear focus as to who would comprise His body.

He conceived of His Son as a Savior, and He determined the ones who needed to be saved—no, who *wanted* to be saved—no, who *would* be saved.

If election is the question, Jesus is the answer. He is its scope and boundary, its basis and purpose. He doesn't have limited capacity to save people. Nor does He have (thank Him) any restriction in His love that excludes some while enfolding others.

An infant born to a teenager is the doorway to the Sanctuary, and though the doorway is narrow, anyone who so desires can fit through it. Anyone truly knocking on the door finds that God had long ago chosen him or her to enter. The mystery is as deep as God is great.

*Chosen in Him*—that simple expression answers the dilemma of who will dwell in the Sanctuary of the Savior.

*Chosen in Him*—it explains how the door opens.

*Chosen in Him*—it is God's unabashed response to all who claim unfairness or prejudice.

*Chosen in Him*—it makes those who are favored fall to their knees in humble gratitude.

## The Perfect Fit

Like I said, God doesn't apologize at all for the apparent conflict between election and free will. In fact, if you take a peek ahead you'll find another head-scratcher: predestination. And we find this duo—"chosen" and "predestined"—again in verse 11: "In him we were also chosen, having been predestined…"

My point is this: God doesn't prefer to keep this doctrine in the closet. He's proud of it. He repeats it over and over as if to say, "See how much I love you?"

And then, as if in the same breath, God says, "whosoever will may come." God doesn't want *anyone* to perish but desires that *all* come to repentance (2 Peter 3:9). We could analyze the chosen/predestined issue to pieces, but I believe that, too often, as we seek to unravel this mystery we lose the wonder of it. Instead, could it be that the point of the whole anomaly is just that: the wonder, the bigness of God that leads to worship?

For now, it is not for us to fully understand the seeming incongruity of election and free will. God desires of us something greater than understanding. He asks us to believe that *He* understands how the two fit together. Perhaps the following parable will illustrate God's desire for us to trust Him in this.

A wise old woman took a young girl on a long hike into the hills where they entered a cave. The woman told the girl to help her dig in the dirt on the cave floor. After they had dug a deep hole, the woman uncovered a sparkling gem that filled her small hand. The gem was shaped like the moon, only cut in half. The spherical side was as smooth as glass while the flat surface was ragged and sharp. After the woman and the girl had enjoyed looking at the half-moon treasure, the old woman returned it to the bottom of the hole and covered it up again.

Then she told the young girl to follow her out of the cave. The two walked through a deep ravine, forded a river, and climbed some hills beyond. Soon, the woman motioned for the girl to follow her into another cave. Again, they dug a hole and, as before, found a sparkling gem shaped like half of a moon. Like the treasure in the first cave, it filled the old woman's hand. It had the same smooth, round surface, and its flat side was jagged. They marveled at the beauty of this gem and after a while buried it again in the cave.

The woman and the girl then returned to the village. The girl asked the elderly woman, "Do the two gems fit together?"

"Yes. They always have, and always will."

"How do you know?"

"Because they are mine. I know they fit together perfectly."

"Then why don't we bring them both into the village and have a celebration?"

"Soon, but not just yet."

The girl persisted. "Why not now?"

"Do you believe they fit together?" the old woman asked.

"Well, yes, but only because you say so."

"Good. That pleases me greatly."

*H*ave you ever considered what it would be like to fully understand God? "Heavenly!" you say. "That's what I want more than anything else!"

I wonder. Think about it. If you could fully understand God, He would be your equal. He could never surprise you with something you didn't previously know. If you and God were mental equals, you could debate God on points of theology and occasionally even win.

Some people give the impression that they would love such a scenario, but I think it would be awful. If God is on my level, then He surely isn't God. If we're equals, then the humanists and hedonists are right when they say that the best path to heaven is education and the best path to hell is pleasure.

But they're not right. You and God aren't peers. He has many truths locked in the secrecy of His greater mind, such as election and free will. You and I will go to our graves picturing them as two half-moon gems, each individually beautiful but resting in separate caves. But on the other side, God will hold a gorgeous, perfect sphere, and when we see it we'll simply say, "Of course!"

## Doctrine in Denim

I hope you'll excuse me for being so personal in this chapter. (I'll try not to let it happen again.) But I want to share with you two brief experiences to make this high and majestic doctrine of God's choosing love accessible, at least inasmuch as it's possible to do so.

Last week I had one of those days. The potential for anger that normally hides deep within me was boiling near the surface. I was a grumpy, middle-aged man. I chewed out my kids most of the day. I was testy with my wife.

I took a long walk, thinking it would help. It didn't. Since it was Saturday, I had the freedom to take a nap, and I did, but still no improvement. Finally, I decided to have mercy on my poor family and go to bed early.

The next morning, with a bit of rest and reasonableness under my belt, I could talk it over with the Lord. Our conversation went something like this...

"Lord, yesterday was terrible. I was such a dragon. Is it the stress I've been under? I hate it when I can't hide the fact that my sinful nature is still very real and very vile."

And since I had been thinking about how God chose people for the Sanctuary, my prayer-dialogue continued...

"Lord, I'm not worthy to be in the Sanctuary."

*I know that, Bob.*

"Then why did You choose me?"

*I didn't know you were going to be this bad.* (This was a joke. God seems to joke with me in my prayers.)

"So, Lord, You don't regret having chosen me?"

*No. That's why I chose you from before the foundation of the world. I wanted you to know that I didn't choose you based on how well you perform. I chose you because it delighted me to do so.*

My friend, you (like me) are so important to God that He put in a special order for you as early as He could!

You have hang-ups, right? You've let Him down and riled Him up, right? God knows that you keep circling back and covering the same old territory, learning the same old lessons. He was aware of your "flight pattern" before He chose you. And it doesn't faze Him.

His choice still stands. And that's no joke.

Hence my second personal illustration. My wife forces me to take these huge pills called B complex. I know she does this because she loves me; she also enjoys poking fun at me as I jerk back my head to get the pills to jump off my tongue cliff down to my stomach's depths. This capsule is supposed to reduce the stress in my life. But actually I've found a better antidote for the stress mess: the doctrine of election.

Case in point: Yesterday my missionary teammates and I sat in a circle in my living room to plan our ministry activities for the upcoming year. We place a lot of importance on these planning meetings because we don't want to waste our time and energy on unproductive activity. As a result, we sometimes put too much pressure on ourselves to develop the plan to beat all plans. I'm embarrassed to admit that, to listen to us, you might think that the world's salvation would be seriously jeopardized without our efforts.

That's probably why the Lord led us to this same passage yesterday morning, for it contains an effective reminder of where we fit in the grand scheme of things: "He chose us in him before the creation of the world." One of my teammates commented that we are often amazed at scriptural statements about being knit together in our mother's womb or called of God from birth, but the fact is God thought about us long before our little bodies altered our mothers' anatomy.

As we discussed this, I noticed a change in the atmosphere of our meeting. Shoulders relaxed, voices grew calmer. Suddenly, we didn't feel so pressured to save the world on our own, for we had a sovereign Savior who has tended to the problem from the beginning of time.

Fellow traveler, what burdens you today? How long is your list of troubles? To dwell in the Sanctuary means to enjoy the loving care of the One who knew you and loved you and chose you before you even knew yourself. Long before Bethlehem, before the world even began, God fixed the commitment of His heart on you—*you!* Your list of concerns can't begin to match God's list of blessings. And your reasons for worry can't stand up to God's reasons for you to be calm—and confident.

Biblical truth, taken regularly, is a great stress reducer. Sometimes it may be a bit hard to swallow, but at least you don't have to jerk your head.

## A Match Made for Heaven

Did you know that the Hebrew word used in the Old Testament for *sanctuary* can also be translated "sacred place" or "holy place"? There's a good reason for this: It is built on an earlier word for "sanctify" or "holy."[1] In other words, the very name *sanctuary* suggests its most dominant characteristic: It is a place of holiness.

Reenter insecurity. (All the doubts of a seven-year-old boy come back to mind.) If the Sanctuary is a place for holy people, then none of us qualify. We feel the same way King David felt: "Lord, who may dwell in your sanctuary? Who may live on your holy hill?" (Psalm 15:1).

But listen closely to the Sanctuary worship: "He chose us in him before the creation of the world to be holy and blameless in his sight." We were chosen to be *holy* and *blameless.* Ring the bell! Sound the gong! God didn't choose us because we were *already* holy and blameless. He chose us that we might *become* holy and blameless in His sight!

The Sanctuary isn't the place where God decided to gather holy people. It is where He chose to gather people to make them holy. In other words, God had a *purpose* in His choosing. He desired to surround His Son with people like His Son—holy people. And to do that he actually separated them from the world and placed them in the holy life of His holy Son. And as a statement of real faith, God gave us a name that shows His commitment to our holiness: *saints,* which means "holy ones."[2] Holiness is God's highest desire, and the creation of a holy people His grandest work.

God chose you because He saw the potential of a holy you. And He's no quitter. God is more committed to your holiness than you are. He is less daunted by failure than you'll ever be. He'll never be sideswiped, bushwhacked, or hoodwinked in His determination to produce greater purity in your heart and mind.

When Joseph caught the newborn infant and said to Mary, "No surprises, honey. It's a boy!" God the Father had already been thinking marriage for what seemed like forever. Like any good father who wants the best for his child, God thought about the qualities necessary for His only Son's mate. The most essential attribute to this particular Father was holiness. That way His Son and His Son's bride would be a perfect match, with no in-law conflicts. Bride and groom would live together in their holy tent, forever.

And so God chose for His Son a bride, long before that Son even appeared on earth. It stretches the imagination a bit, but it's a thought-provoking fact: The untold story of Bethlehem is that the infant Jesus was already engaged!

Which means that you and I are already spoken for.

*Lord, may I confide in You for a moment?*

*I've always had a nickname for myself. Never told anyone else.*

*Never even thought of telling anyone till just now.*

*My secret name for myself is "Unspecial." That's me, the way I see me.*

*Plain face in a boring crowd.*

*Others would protest, claiming my specialness.*

But my heart has become accustomed to the old nickname.

It fits.

Still, I'm beginning to wonder if I've misnamed myself.

Feelings aside, it seems You have a different opinion of me.

So I might try on some new names.

"Chosen" has a nice ring to it. I'm rather partial to "Select" as well.

Or maybe "His."

Yes, the more I think about it, the more I'm convinced I need a new name.

Anything but "Unspecial."

But then, You've already taken care of that, haven't You?

# The Highlight of His Day

*The rambunctious lad jumped from the car*
*before it came to a full stop.*
*Watching from the car, his parents beamed*
*as their hair-tossed son ran down the sidewalk toward his buddies*
*with the good news.*
*His tie knocked askew, his little blazer by now tossed aside,*
*the boy ran straight into his crowd of expectant friends*
*with the announcement*
*he had waited so long to give:*
*"Hey, I got adopted!"*

There once was a baby boy born to a Jewish family. The birth happened in transit, after which events quickly turned for the worse and the family found themselves refugees in a distant land called Egypt. Living as strangers and aliens was not easy; it never is. But the experience drew the family closer together. From the beginning, their love for one another grew stronger and stronger.

Every night, Joseph left the workshop he was renting. (It was actually nothing more than an open place under a tree near the market.) As quickly as possible, he returned home and cleaned himself from the day of working with wood and tools. Expectantly, he put on clean clothes, making sure to wear something soft. He lovingly greeted his wife, Mary, then invariably and non-verbally, his widening eyes asked, "Where is He?" You see, the highlight of Joseph's day was the moment he could hold his son in his strong hands.

Every evening, Joseph sat in a comfortable chair and cradled the infant

Jesus in his arms. He talked to Jesus in what would have appeared to anyone else as a one-way conversation, but Joseph knew he was reaching his son. He told his son about his day, about the jobs he was working on, about the interesting people he had met. As he spoke, Joseph always used the family's native language so the lad could someday understand his own people back in Galilee.

Joseph wondered when Jesus would begin to speak. Until then, he enjoyed the gurgling and cooing sounds that emitted from the sometimes-slurping smile of his tiny apprentice. The baby's little eyes sparkled as He looked into His father's. He snuggled into the warmth of His father's muslin-clothed arms. He seemed fascinated by speech, sometimes transfixed as His father's mouth formed the sounds and syllables of the day's events.

The baby listened intently, apparently understanding His father's description of their future life in Nazareth, and of the workshop—a proper one—they would share when they returned home.

It happened one evening as Joseph told his little son about that night in Bethlehem when the stars seemed brighter than usual. For the hundredth time, he told his little lad their private joke about how easy Mary had it—how offering her the donkey made the long trip from Nazareth a cinch for her—chuckling once again as he tried to convince his attentive baby that the real credit should go to the father, squeamish about blood yet stepping in as midwife to welcome the special infant from Mary's womb.

Joseph paused in his storytelling, pondering again that chilly night. That was when the baby said His first word.

I suppose it's no surprise what the infant said.

And I suppose Joseph's workmates, all the way from Egypt to Nazareth, never heard the end of it.

For what the baby said, with twinkling eyes and gurgling smile, was "Abba."

## Your First Word

I'm using my imagination, of course. We don't know for sure the first word of Jesus, for Scripture does not record it. The mother tongue Joseph and Mary would have used at home was their native dialect, Galilean Aramaic. That's why it isn't a stretch to guess that Jesus' first word might have been "Abba," for it is the Aramaic word for *Father*. In fact, *Abba* is the intimate kind of word you would call a dearly loved father, so we could rightly translate it "Daddy" or "Papa."[1]

Here's where it gets good: *Abba* is a part of *our* vocabulary too:

> But when the fulness of the time came, God sent forth His Son, born of a woman, born under the Law, in order that He might redeem those who were under the Law, that we might receive the adoption as sons. And because you are sons, God has sent forth the Spirit of His Son into our hearts, crying, "Abba! Father!" (Galatians 4:4–6, NASB)

"Abba." It's the sentiment that the believer instinctively cries out to the Father. We have a yearning for intimacy with God, and for good reason. Our relationship with God is more than servants to master, even more than worshipers to worshiped one. No, what draws us toward intimacy with God is that we belong to His family.

Think through that verse again. When the Father knew the timing was just right, He sent His eternal Son to be born into time. Why? So that many people born into time might be born into eternity.

The best earthly metaphor to describe this heavenly mystery is adoption. Notice that the adoption makes our standing in God's family a fact: "God sent forth His Son...that we might receive the adoption as sons. And *because* you are sons, God has sent forth the Spirit of His Son into our hearts, crying, "Abba! Father!" (Galatians 4:4–6, NASB, emphasis mine).

But there's more. God seemingly wanted us to have the *feeling* of being adopted. How could He help us feel that we truly belong to His family? How could He make our status as His children more than words on a page?

By doing something phenomenal, something only He could do. To help us feel and experience the safety, warmth, and protection of being His children, He put within us the Spirit of His own Son, Jesus Christ.

The human delight of a baby gazing at his carpenter father's smile was but a reflection of God the Son's eternal yearning for God the Father: "Abba!" And the Spirit of that eternal yearning has been placed permanently in the soul of every adopted child of God: "Abba, I need you. I love you. I long for you. I delight in you!"

I have no Bible reference for this, but I would argue that the first words, at least the first sentiment, of every new believer is "Abba! Father!" And I'll go further: The heart of an adopted believer yearning for God is the best assurance of salvation and the greatest blessing of Sanctuary life. So many people (myself included) want greater intimacy with God, knowing He is present but yearning to know Him better, to feel His love.

Yearning for God is a gift! It is the Spirit of Jesus within us, crying out insatiably for our heavenly Father. We cannot truly rest until we are in our Father's bosom, feeling His warm embrace, listening to His sonorous voice, watching the glistening of His eyes, and looking into the joy of His sacred smile.

We're not orphans anymore.

Someone cared about us.

Someone chose us.

Hey, we got adopted!

## No Consolation Prize

It's not at all surprising that they now sing about it in the Sanctuary: "In love he predestined us to be adopted as his sons through Jesus Christ, in accordance with his pleasure and will" (Ephesians 1:4–5).

The word for *adoption* is one of those explicit words that doesn't require much explanation. It consists of the word for *son* put together with a word for *placing*. So it literally means "a placing as a son."[2]

Lyn and I have been blessed with two children, both daughters. One came to us by biological birth while the other was "placed" in our home by adoption. I have to say that we love each of them uniquely and equally.

Being adoptive parents has taught us many things, not the least of which is other people's profound misunderstanding of adoption. Rather than seeing it as an incredible adventure and desirable choice, many people seem to think adoption is a consolation prize for those willing to settle for it. This attitude was reflected in some of the statements made to us by well-meaning but ignorant folks:

"Maybe after you adopt you'll be able to have a child of your own."

*I know what you mean, but do you really think we'll consider this child as some kind of houseguest?*

"I couldn't adopt. I could never love someone else's child."

*Is biological birth the only way to really enter a family?*

"If the child you adopt turns out to be diseased or deformed, can you give it back?"

*I can't believe you said that! If your biological child were born diseased or deformed, would you give him or her back?*

If you have this "second-best" view of adoption, then you probably don't understand what adoption means in the Bible. If you think that God couldn't have a *real* family any other way except adoption, then you can't comprehend the incredible first-choice kind of love He has for you. And should you consider it possible that God would give you back if you turn up with a disease or deformity of heart or body, then you undoubtedly suffer from insecurity in your relationship with your heavenly Father.

This ought not be so, for adoption in the Sanctuary isn't a runner-up trophy. Speaking as an adoptive father, I can tell you this: There is a special love between a parent and an adopted child.

Let me confide in you transparently for a moment. Two times in my life I've become so choked up with emotion that I literally couldn't force myself to speak. (Embarrassingly, both were occasions when I was expected to say something!) The first happened the day we went to the courthouse to sign the legal papers making Lauren's adoption official. This event followed nine months of home inspections by social workers and various legal hurdles we had to overcome. After we left the courthouse where we had met with the judge (I recall him saying something such as "I wish all my duties were as pleasant as this one"), we went to a nearby restaurant to celebrate. My parents were there. Lyn's parents were there. Our lawyer friend was there. We talked and laughed and passed our new daughter around for everyone to enjoy. And did we enjoy her! How good God had been! After seven years of longing for a biological child but being unable to have one, Lyn and I rejoiced that God had graced our nest with new life.

I asked that we pray and thank Him. I began, "Dear heavenly Father..."
and I don't think I progressed much beyond that. The tremendous relief of
finalizing the adoption completely overwhelmed me. (As I recall, Lyn had to
finish that prayer for me.)

My teammates in Kenya could tell you about the second time I was overcome with emotion. It happened about ten years later. We were on a team
retreat (a time to come *away* from our busy ministry activity to avoid coming
*apart* because of it). As we occasionally do, we were praying for our children.
On that particular day, I chose to pray for Lauren. I began, "Dear heavenly
Father..." and followed it with a long (and I mean long!) period of silence. I
couldn't speak. Meanwhile, God was replaying in my mind the miracle of
Lauren's adoption. Patiently my teammates waited. And waited. My memory
was flooded with all the angst and frustration and relief and joy that Lyn and I
had experienced:

> ...how we had tried to adopt an emotionally abused boy thirteen years ear-
> lier but with great difficulty decided against it because we knew we
> would soon move to an unknown destination;
> ...how, a year later, we endured the whole legal and emotional process of
> adopting a boy but ended up empty-handed in a courtroom because the
> foster parents decided at the last moment to adopt the child themselves;
> ...how my father wrote to all the obstetric doctors in his town, asking
> them to consider his son and wife as adoption recipients;
> ...how a Christian doctor actually responded (we know and love him to
> this day);
> ...how we received a phone call at 6:00 A.M. one Saturday and drove for six
> excited hours to pick up God's gift to us when she was just two hours old.

Can you blame an adoptive father for being overcome with relief and gratitude and hopes and dreams? Thankfully my teammates didn't. (I think Lyn had
to finish that prayer too!)

I believe our heavenly Father feels just as deeply about adoption. I think He
knows, on a much deeper level than Lyn and I and a million other adoptive par-

ents, the relief and gratitude and hopes and dreams for His adoptive children. He knows that you, like most adopted children, were born in adverse circumstances; that you, like most adopted children, face an uphill climb; that you, like most adopted children, joined the family by an extraordinary string of miracles, producing a unique kind of love!

When she was young, Heather (our second daughter, the one born to us biologically) would sometimes be afraid at night, as all kids are at times. When this happened, she instinctively cried out, "Daddy! Mommy!" This is the natural thing for children to do. Whenever Lauren was in trouble or afraid, she had a reaction that was just as predictable: She cried out, "Daddy! Mommy!" She has the same instinct, and rightfully so. It has never occurred to her to reason like this: *It's dark and I'm afraid. I'd like to call out to my daddy, but since I'm adopted I'm not sure if I should.*

Similarly, neither Lyn nor I have ever lain in our bed at night and had this thought: *Did I just hear one of the girls call out for me? Which one was it? Oh, it was just Lauren. I'm so tired. Can't get up. She'll be okay.*

No loving adoptive parent thinks like that. I know God doesn't. Your cries for help never fall on deaf ears. He sought you and bought you, knew you and drew you. Believe me, He'll never ignore you. Never be too busy. Never roll over and muffle His ears with a pillow. He's your *Abba.*

## Patermouthis, Age Two

The Holy Spirit chose the apostle Paul to reveal the most compelling truth about the believer's adoption into God's family. This was not a coincidence. Paul, though Jewish by ethnicity, possessed Roman citizenship and broad knowledge of the Roman world (Acts 16:37; 22:25). We could basically describe him as a Jewish lawyer (Acts 22:3), and he was probably also familiar with Roman law, having that frame of mind anyway.

Therefore, when we read Paul's proclamations about adoption, we can safely assume that he reflected the current thinking of his day about that transaction. And since Roman law dominated the known world during this time period, the Roman view of adoption helps us understand our adoption and our life in the Sanctuary.

With that in mind, let's look at an actual adoption contract from the ancient Roman world. It was written and enacted in A.D. 335, and accurately reflects Roman adoption law as practiced when Paul lived and wrote. As you read the content of this ancient document, look for characteristics of adoption.

> We acknowledge, Heracles and his wife Isarion on the one side, that we have given to you, Horion, for adoption our son Patermouthis, aged about two years, and I, Horion, on the other side, that I have taken him as my true son, so as to establish for him the rights of succession to my estate; and it shall not be lawful for me to disavow him or reduce him to slavery, because he is well-born and of well-born and free parents; and likewise it shall not be lawful for us, Heracles and his wife Isarion, to remove the boy from you, Horion, because we have once for all given him away to you for adoption, nor shall it hereafter be lawful for anyone to transgress the terms of the deed, because on these we have consented and agreed.[3]

This little contract protected two-year-old Patermouthis (I wonder if Horion changed his name!) in some big ways. Two kinds of guarantees stand out to me:

1. *Full privileges and inheritance*—reflected in the words "true son" and "rights of succession to my estate"; and
2. *Permanency/finality*—evident in the phrases "it shall not be lawful for me to disavow him or reduce him to slavery" and "it shall not be lawful for us...to remove the boy from you...because we have once for all given him away to you for adoption."

In one way, your heart has to go out to little Patermouthis because you wonder how Heracles and Isarion decided to give him up. Isarion wasn't a single mother unable to keep the little guy. And they obviously weren't struggling financially, for they were "well-born and free parents." Courts today probably would not grant the adoption in this case, citing it as unwarranted. But the

Romans obviously believed in and practiced a strong form of adoption. And Horion, perhaps a single man, would now have a son and an heir.

Now, consider the case of another Father in search of children to inherit His estate. Notice the same qualities in the contract He has drawn up for them.

### GOD's ADOPTION CONTRACT

For you did not receive a spirit that makes you a slave again to fear, but you received the Spirit of sonship. And by him we cry, "Abba, Father." The Spirit himself testifies with our spirit that we are God's children. Now if we are children, then we are heirs—heirs of God and co-heirs with Christ, if indeed we share in his sufferings in order that we may also share in his glory. (Romans 8:15–17)

But when the time had fully come, God sent his Son, born of a woman, born under law, to redeem those under law, that we might receive the full rights of sons. Because you are sons, God sent the Spirit of his Son into our hearts, the Spirit who calls out, "Abba, Father." So you are no longer a slave, but a son; and since you are a son, God has made you also an heir. (Galatians 4:4–7)

Let's rejoice in the details of *our* contract. *Full privileges and inheritance* are reflected in the following words:

- "The Spirit himself testifies with our spirit that we are God's children" (Romans 8:16);
- "Now if we are children, then we are heirs—heirs of God and co-heirs with Christ" (Romans 8:17);
- "the full rights of sons" (Galatians 4:5);
- "since you are a son, God has made you also an heir" (Galatians 4:7).

*Permanency/finality* is evident in these phrases:

- "you received the Spirit of sonship" (Romans 8:15; *sonship* is the same Greek word often translated "adoption");
- "you are no longer a slave, but a son" (Galatians 4:7).

We can also rest assured that in Christ adoption is not a male thing. Though Paul uses the masculine *son* in the metaphor of Roman adoption, he makes it clear that God adopted into His family children of both genders. He wrote a kind of preamble to the adoption contract that reflects the gender and ethnic diversity of God's adopting action: "You are all sons of God through faith in Christ Jesus, for all of you who were baptized into Christ have clothed your-selves with Christ. There is neither Jew nor Greek, slave nor free, male nor female, for you are all one in Christ Jesus" (Galatians 3:26–28).

During every day, and stretching through every night, the Spirit of God tes-tifies to your spirit, whispering to your heart, saying, "You are God's child. You are God's child" (Romans 8:16). This soft message reverberates continually through everyone who has been escorted into the Sanctuary.[4]

For now, we must be content with these quiet whispers of our standing as God's children. But one day our hope will bear fruit in the physical and heavenly realization of the adoption God has already accomplished: "Not only so, but we ourselves, who have the firstfruits of the Spirit, groan inwardly as we wait eagerly for our adoption as sons, the redemption of our bodies" (Romans 8:23).

The Sanctuary, for the time being, is a place of *faith* whereby we agree with God, saying, "Yes, I am God's child." One day relatively soon, it will be a place of *sight* where we will declare, "Wow, I *am* God's child!"

## What Parent and Child Need

Almost without exception, the process of adoption requires that a particular function be performed. It is the function of *agency.*

Now, I realize that we've all had experiences in which the terms *agency* and *action* were unrelated! But, theoretically, agencies and agents are those groups or individuals who make things happen.

In the process of adoption, in its simplest form, two parties need action. The parent seeks a child, and the child needs a parent. (In some situations more parties are involved, such as the parent or guardian giving up the child for adop-tion.)

What the seeking parent and the needy child require is an agent, someone who can connect or link them together, who can provide a basis for them to become acquainted and establish a relationship, who can provide a proving ground for their compatibility.

To be specific, once God the Father chose you as part of His family, He predestined you to be adopted. But He still needed someone to perform the agency function. He, and we, needed

> …a connecting link;
> …a basis for becoming acquainted and establishing a relationship; and
> …a proving ground for our compatibility.

Yet again, the solution to the dilemma proved to be a Person. The means by which we orphans became linked with the God who desired us was brought under that Person's control. We were brought into the Sanctuary of Jesus. Watch for our Agent in the hymn's lyrics as the choirs sing tirelessly of Him: "In love he predestined us to be adopted as his sons *through Jesus Christ*"(Ephesians 1:4–5, emphasis mine).

*T*he absolute cruciality of Jesus continues to be reinforced, doesn't it? For the third time in this first hymn, we hear that our whole existence before God is wrapped inexplicably in and through the life of Christ:

> We have every spiritual blessing *in Christ;*
> God chose us *in Him;*
> and now,
> we are adopted *through Christ.*

The adoption Agent has worked on the Father's behalf to convey to us His love. Notice this function showing through in Jesus' prayer in the upper room:

> Righteous Father, though the world does not know you, I know you, and they [the believers] know that you have sent me. *I have made you*

*known to them, and will continue to make you known* in order that the love you have for me may be in them and that I myself may be in them. (John 17:25–26, emphasis mine)

And Jesus is *our* agent too, providing us the basis for becoming acquainted with the Father and being brought into His family: "Yet to all who received him, to those who believed in his name, *he gave the right to become children of God*—children born not of natural descent, nor of human decision or a husband's will, but born of God" (John 1:12–13, emphasis mine).

Do you want to understand how God ensured that His love for you wouldn't go unexpressed? He invested the responsibility with a reliable man, His Son. To fill the role of adoption agent, Jesus had to stoop low enough to meet us on our level, so He became one of us.

*I*n adoption agencies around the world, books on shelves, in a sense, hold the destiny of children of all ages. Each page has a picture of a child, the child's name, his or her age, his or her interests, his or her needs. Parents looking to adopt come and pore over those books. In one way you'd think, "What could they possibly tell from one of those pictures? How could they possibly make such a major decision based on the sketchy information on those pages?"

Yet I've heard that an amazing thing often happens. As a couple leafs through those picture books, page after page, book after book, they come to a particular page containing the picture of a particular child. They pause. They look at each other, nodding. And they say, "That's the one!"

For a moment, turn on your imagination and look around the Sanctuary. See those people? They aren't dignitaries or notables. They—we!—are ordinary folks, born in adverse circumstances, facing an uphill climb. The Father leafed through the annals of His creation, page by page, and joyfully said, "That's the one!" and "That's the one!" and again and again He predestined us to adoption as His children. As John, called "the disciple whom Jesus loved," wrote, "How great is the love the Father has lavished on us, that we should be called children of God! And that is what we are!" (1 John 3:1).

I don't know if the Sanctuary has a fireplace, but I know it's filled with warmth.

I don't know if it has the smell of home-cooked food, but I know it has the pleasing aroma of the Father.

And I don't know if I can *like* everyone else in the Sanctuary, but I do know that every single one of us belongs there, because long ago God thought of each one and said, "That's the one!"

*Abba, Father,*

*Could you hold me in Your strong arms like You held Jesus?*

*I need to smell Your smell, to gaze into Your warm eyes.*

*I long to hear Your voice telling me of hopes and dreams*

*You hold in Your heart for me.*

*Thank You for sparing no expense in finding the one*

*Agent who could bring us together.*

*Thank You for replacing my empty life with the full privileges of adoption.*

*And thank You that by Your gracious love,*

*I am the highlight of Your day!*

# *Selah*
# *Bethlehem*

*Selah (Hebrew): to rest, indicating either the pause of the voice in singing so that only instruments are heard, or a break in the psalm where there is a call to rest and reflect on the preceding words*
*Bethlehem (Hebrew): literally, "house of bread"; a town in Judea, 7 kilometers or about 4.5 miles south of Jerusalem, the home of David, hence the birthplace of the Messiah[1]*

*C*hances are it didn't come up in the morning gossip at the bread shop the next day. The innkeeper likely offered no apology. You see, ordinary events rarely make headlines.

We've idealized Jesus' birth so thoroughly that we imagine it must have caused a real stir throughout Bethlehem. Not so. To be sure, the shepherds told all their friends, but by most accounts it was just another birth to another poor family in yet one more overcrowded town. Rather like the hundreds of babies born each day in the slums of today's overstuffed cities.

I would guess that the first thing Jesus smelled was cattle urine mixed with the bittersweet odors of aging hay, dirt, dung, and chicken corn. Though He was completely divine, Jesus was also fully human. I surmise therefore that Mary's newborn ran the typical out-of-hospital risks of infection or of picking up a chill. I wonder if He was jaundiced.

The birth was also pretty much a private affair, as they often are. Father, mother, child, goats, chickens… It must have been lonely. Mary hadn't experienced this before. Neither had Joseph. I don't read of any midwife helping. And where were the relatives? Every single one of Joseph's relatives were supposed to participate in the same census that brought Joseph to Bethlehem. Granted, Mary's mother and sisters were reporting to their husbands' towns, but didn't Joseph have a sister or aunt who could have lent a helping hand? Wasn't something amiss here?

I wonder if the relatives stayed away. I know that Aunt Elizabeth and her husband supported the young couple from Nazareth, but they had the benefit of insight from God. The others could only go on appearances, and appearances weren't good. A girl pregnant so soon? And so secretive about it? Didn't look good at all.

Maybe this birth did reach beyond the ordinary. Maybe it was actually inglorious.

Next time you set out those figurines of Joseph and Mary, shepherds, sheep, and wise men (who never actually came to the manger), consider that couple's raw courage. Think of how, from many angles, Jesus' birth was plain and ordinary.

But don't stop there. Remember that appearances can be deceiving.

Certainly, angels never gave such public performances at any other birth. They're probably still talking about that night outside of Bethlehem ("Remember the way those sheep just froze, then bolted in a thousand different directions?"). And how often does an angel make a personal appearance to the expectant father and mother? How would you feel if an angel said of your son, "his kingdom will never end" (Luke 1:33)?

Then there was the day Mary's relative Elizabeth greeted her by saying, "Blessed are you among women, and blessed is the child you will bear! But why am I so favored, that the mother of my Lord should come to me?" (Luke 1:42–43). Mary knew no other pregnancy could ever match her first.

And those shepherds. You know, the ones whose glassy-eyed sheep were still scattered over three square miles? Don't they point to the unusual? I can't imagine Joseph glossing over their arrival too nonchalantly: "Hi, fellows. Just passing through the barn? You guys lose a sheep or something?" No, those shepherds were ecstatic! They had seen a heavenly display fit for kings.

To be sure, the chronicle of that starry night transcends the logistics of the Christmas play. There is a fuller tale, one that includes you. The story often left untold is that an ordinary birth in Bethlehem linked heaven and earth. A first-born son was given to a carpenter, but a family was being born to God Himself. The infant lying on hay would enable God to pour the entire treasure chest of heaven on His many sons and daughters.

If you took every piece of straw in that manger and made it a string of pearls...

If you took each calf and cow and goat and turned them into solid gold of the best quality...

If you changed each granule of dirt into a diamond, and transformed the acrid stench into the fragrance of the finest perfume...

You would not even begin to match the real wealth in the manger that day.

That baby wasn't actually poor at all.

Isn't it about time we stopped believing the lies? You know, the ones about our worthlessness? About our poverty of soul? I say it's time to lay down the gauntlet of truth. To declare to heaven and earth that we are God's children and proud of it. Chosen for holiness. Predestined in love. Adopted because it pleased God.

Fact is, the coming of Jesus was a lavish display. Even gold and diamonds couldn't tell the half.

# Second

# Hymn

# The Hidden Hope of Golgotha
## Our Deliverance in the Son

In him we have redemption through his blood,

the forgiveness of sins,

in accordance with the riches of God's grace

that he lavished on us with all wisdom and understanding.

And he made known to us the mystery of his will

according to his good pleasure, which he purposed in Christ,

to be put into effect when the times

will have reached their fulfillment——to bring all things

in heaven and on earth

together under one head, even Christ.

In him we were also chosen,

having been predestined

according to the plan of him who works out everything

in conformity with the purpose of his will,

in order that we, who were the first to hope in Christ,

might be for the praise of his glory.

EPHESIANS 1:7–12

How little we knew that when Jesus died
He poured out so much forgiveness
that it's still spilling over.

*"On a hill far away*
*stood an old rugged cross,*
*the emblem of suff'ring and shame...."*

*E*very town has its "bad side," where people reside only if they must, and upstanding citizens visit with trepidation if they visit it at all. You undoubtedly know the kinds of places I mean. In your town, it might be a row of taverns that belch forth lasciviousness and violence. Maybe there's a place by a river or up in the hills where malcontents meet after dark to do dark deeds. Perhaps it's a place where a violent act occurred, such as an abandoned home where a husband once shot his wife.

Such places existed in ancient Jerusalem as well. One we know about was called the Field of Blood, where strangers were typically buried. This is where someone apparently buried Judas's shamed carcass after he hanged himself.[1] There was also a ravine south of town called the Valley of Hinnom, where people sacrificed children to the god Molech.[2]

But the ultimate place of shame was called Golgotha. It was an execution site, and Jesus' destiny aimed straight for it.

One wonders about that place's history. Jerusalem, of course, is an ancient city dating back to the Bronze Age, and King David elevated it to notoriety. But how long had Golgotha been a place of death? Surely violent men had for centuries earned the death penalty. How many of them paid that price at Golgotha? Did this place have a millennium-long legacy of shameful death?

The mind wonders. How many wives and lovers later returned to Golgotha to view the mournful site in silence and let their tears flow? How many children came back the next week or year or decade and wondered what might have been, searching their minds for even the faintest memory of who their criminal fathers really were?

Did some people lose their lives on Golgotha unjustly? How many lost their future because they were skillfully framed, thanks to a jealous relative or vengeful business partner? How much false evidence escorted innocents to that hill? Were there men who found their way to the cross because of a political feud, or refugees who met their death because they showed up in the wrong part of town with the wrong color skin? Did Golgotha host men who had endured round after round of appeals, only ultimately to die because lazy officials were too tired to review the case just one more time? How many of those men had every vestige of hope wrenched from their grasp?

I wonder if there were Golgotha groupies who never missed an execution. They would have been the peculiar types who brought picnic lunches, morbid men seeking perverted thrills and propelled by a twisted sense of entertainment.

As you ponder all of this, you might also wonder: How many demons lived on that hill? The unseen world holds a host of mysteries, but one we now understand is that evil spirits crave destruction and death. How many spirits of ruin stationed themselves on Golgotha?

And what about the soldiers? Were they professional executioners merely fulfilling their task from a sense of duty? Did they disdain their indecent assignment, wishing no one had to do a job like that? Or did some of them actually request transfer to the Golgotha detail? Maybe some of them especially enjoyed the ethnic jobs, relishing the chance to put an Arab or Jew to death. Perhaps they viewed it as a bonus to put a Samaritan, or even an African, up to the wood.

We know there was a lucrative side to the assignment. We read in Scripture that Golgotha soldiers gambled for Jesus' clothing. Maybe some convicts managed to hang on to a piece of jewelry until the moment they were nailed to the cross, a ring given by a father or a necklace received from a friend. How much outright theft took place on the shameful hill just outside Jerusalem, the so-called "City of Peace"?

*I*f God had announced that the hope of salvation was staked on Golgotha, the whole host of humankind would have laughed in united mockery. There was no conceivable way that any good could come from that wretched place. No one ever showed mercy there, only vengeance. Never forgiveness, only hate. It was a rock with no redeeming value.

Golgotha was nicknamed "Skull." Did it receive that nickname because, as some guess, the side of the hill had a pattern of indentations resembling the sunken eyes and nose of a skull? Was it the mere association between death and skeletons that brought the uncomplimentary ascription? Or was it even that skulls were left or returned to the place by hoodlums, adding shame upon shame? Did youths come with mischief in mind, kicking the skulls as if to play a game or stacking them up in mocking monuments to misery or bashing them against the rocks in ignorant imitation of the thousands of lives and families shattered on that shameful protuberance outside Jerusalem?

Indeed, it was a vile place, Golgotha.

Or so you would have thought.

Who would have imagined that that dark, demonically infested mound would receive the glory-infused presence of majesty? Who could have imagined that a place where hopes and dreams were smashed like abandoned craniums against granite would become the very place, the *only* place, where we could find true hope?

> *"And I love that old cross*
> *where the dearest and best*
> *for a world of lost sinners was slain...."*

I've speculated quite a bit about Golgotha, but no one really knows much about it. No one knows its true location, its appearance, the details of its history.

But I know this for certain: A Sanctuary once rested there.

Few understood the immensity of the event. Blithely ignorant of the presence of greatness, sightseers stared their stares and quipped their quips; officials and guards proceeded with their execution protocol just as they had dozens of times before (and dozens yet to come); the gamers and thieves put in a whopping good day of crisp business; the friends and relatives said their good-byes and mourned their losses. But perhaps only God the Father—who just three short years before had said, "This is my beloved son in whom I am well-pleased"[3]—perhaps only He and His Son, the convict—who the very night before had crumpled beside a rock in Gethsemane and cried, "Abba, Father"[4]—

perhaps only they knew that Light had cast out Darkness that day, that Hope had snuck up and caught Despair unaware.

> *"So I'll cherish the old rugged cross,*
> *till my trophies at last I lay down;*
> *I will cling to the old rugged cross,*
> *and exchange it someday for a crown."* [5]

Golgotha.

Isn't it just like Jesus to go to the bad part of town and get rowdy?

That's exactly what He did. He went there one morning, by appointment, and smashed our shame against the granite.

# CHAPTER FOUR

# Devastation

*The most depressing aspect of life Outside is that people there don't want help even when Someone offers it to them.*

As we sang the first hymn of the Sanctuary, we discovered the reality of the Sanctuary blessings and we basked in the incredible privilege that God chose us to be there—that He adopted us into His family as His children.

We now begin singing the second hymn, and it will cause us to rejoice in our deliverance in the Son. But to embrace our deliverance, we need to fully understand the emptiness and death from which God has delivered us. And to understand that, not just academically but emotionally, we need to do something very difficult. We need to take a journey outside the Sanctuary, a journey that will remind us of existence outside of Jesus Christ.

We all will find the scene familiar, for each one of us has been there. We will all recognize the despair outside, for it is the condition into which we were all born.

As you read this chapter, you may be one of those who has yet to be delivered from the kingdom of darkness. May this journey be especially revealing for you.

Before we depart, let me give you a scriptural launch point. You may recall my mentioning earlier that if Paul had laid out his letter to Ephesus in logical order, he would have begun with chapter 2. So let's look at that passage to remember the condition that makes the Sanctuary so necessary. Life without Jesus is concisely expressed in these words.

As for you, you were dead in your transgressions and sins, in which you used to live when you followed the ways of this world and of the ruler of the kingdom of the air, the spirit who is now at work in those who are disobedient. All of us also lived among them at one time, gratifying the cravings of our sinful nature and following its desires and thoughts. Like the rest, we were by nature objects of wrath. (Ephesians 2:1–3)

We are about to visit that sad terrain. Turn around and take one last, long look around the Sanctuary. How does it appear to you? Is it beautifully decorated with carvings and stained-glass windows? Does it have a casual beauty with colorful banners of praise? Listen to the music—hear the voices singing purely. Does a powerful organ or a melodious guitar accompany them?

Linger for a moment and soak up the Sanctuary's strength. (You'll need it through the journey that looms ahead.) Feel the warmth and light and simple pleasantness of the life and presence of Jesus. Breathe in the contentment of belonging to God, of having been adopted forever into His family. Revel in the blessings and the promises that are eternally yours.

I suppose we had better get going; any more delays and we'll likely lose our resolve. Come then, for just a short while, to the kingdom of darkness: Devastation. Learn to appreciate the day by taking a glimpse into the night. Remember life outside of Christ, and be thankful for your rescue.

## Journey to the Land of Wrath

First impressions sometimes linger longest. Such is the case with stepping outside the Sanctuary. The first assault is by the darkness. The dreary cheerlessness hangs like a cloud of gloom. But the shadowy pall represents more than inclement weather, for a dismal and villainous air permeates every den with foreboding.

As your eyes adjust to the darkness, you'll likely realize that it masks an indescribable squalor. Sewage courses under the feet, offering a constant stench to the nostrils while providing nourishment for vermin and breeding grounds for disease. Hunched over in shame, clothed in dreary rags, and bearing the soggy grime of the earth, are human figures. Many weep, some sob, not a few cry out in anguish.

Like the beggar boys in today's slums who travel from scrap heap to scrap heap, gathering overstuffed sacks of old cartons and plastic containers only to hand them over to older boys for some small profit, the poor fools in Devastation cling to worthless treasures that they ultimately cannot keep. Poverty of heart is their terminal disease.

Having just come from the Sanctuary, we can't possibly miss another initial impression: No one is singing. Oh, there's sound: crying, wailing, and the noise you could never become accustomed to hearing—gnashing teeth. Sound but no singing, because no one has a song. Someone could sing a mournful melody perhaps, but even that requires creativity. In this place, despair strangled creativity long ago. In the Land of Wrath, no rock would give a second thought to shouting out praise. The rocks don't even mumble optimistically here. And the tree branches never learned to applaud. No reason to.

But that doesn't mean that worship is totally absent from life Outside. On the contrary. A master rules over this defilement, and he clearly owns the hearts and affections of every hovel of humanity. How every single dejected person could offer allegiance to the villainous lord whom they so thoroughly fear is a mystery shrouded in darkness. Deceived into loving that which they hate, members of this kingdom are beguiled by an unhallowed perversion. The obscenely powerful worship has inconspicuously intruded into every soul.

As if on cue, the atmosphere suddenly plummets from awful to worse. Widened eyes turn to trace the path of a dark figure skulking through the rubble, sniffing for anything that interests him, looking for signs of weakness. It's the roaring lion who rules the Outside. His appearance in the slum instantly exposes the source of his powerful hold: fear.

It is evident that he rarely goes hungry, for the inhabitants of this land are captive to the fear. The lion never returns to his lair until he has stalked and ravaged and gorged. Even the slobber from his twisted mouth drools deception: "I can kill you any time I want, and there is no telling how terrible death will be. Nothing could be worse. And who knows what will come after that. This is all you have. Cling to the now. You see it and know it. It's safe. This is as good as it gets."

The whole kingdom lives in fear of this lurking scavenger. Any who seek to find another way immediately return to submission when reminded of the loathsome thought of death. The master of Devastation holds the ultimate weapon, and his subjects are slaves to his villainous power.[1]

## A Lion's Trophy

She slumps against a wall, her bent frame forbidding an upward glance. Her emotional infrastructure—the basic coping ability that everyone takes for granted—is in shambles.

Many times, others can't see spiritual sickness. It's an inner torment that the victim bears alone, such as the housewife fulfilling her daily duties while battling the constant temptation to walk out or take her life, or the business executive enduring endless days, overcoming the hourly longing to quit the charade. But in the hunched woman's case, something is obviously wrong. Anyone can see it. The spiritual infection has manifested itself physically, for the woman is bent double, debilitated by the demonic. Her posture gives testimony to the lion's cruelty. Her viewpoint is necessarily downcast; her everyday world is the ground before her. Only rarely can she catch a glimpse of a tree or the sky. Her face is forever the target of sniffing dogs and of the dust of walkers hurrying by. It's as if the destroyer has said, "You will crawl on your belly and you will eat dust all the days of your life."[2]

She struggles to keep her hair out of her face. And since she reached her eighteenth year as a cripple, she has found it difficult to find either the strength or the reason to smile.

As he always does, the lion has ravaged the woman's family as well. Perhaps it began with her husband's embarrassment over her condition. As her symptoms became increasingly obvious, her husband found tactful ways to leave her at home from social occasions. He became adept at making excuses for her chronic absence while she grew skillful at resentment and self-pity.

Children are quick learners; before long, hers recognized her dysfunction. Innocently at first, they began joking about her. To ease their embarrassment, they put her down when with their friends, hoping to distance themselves from the distorted lady at home.

Hers is a despicable life, a lion's trophy. No matter how hard she tries, she can't straighten her body or her life.[3]

## Riches to Rags

The man sits in a puddle of muck. "Aah! Go away from me, you stinking vermin! Curse you, filthy licking scoundrel! My sores are not your food. Leave me to the flies and return to your putrid vomit!"

The rags he now wears were once a fine, three-piece, pinstripe suit. "Someone get these dogs away from me!"

What's really pathetic is his helplessness. He can't even defend himself against the hounding curs, because both of his arms cling to his precious "treasures." He has spent his whole life gathering them: flattened cartons, tin cans, plastic jars without caps. Holding on to them has made his posture awkward and pitiful.

He speaks gibberish. The sight of the chasm has driven him to the brink of madness. ("Murja Lazarus djou beeja firshy kaga...!") Stubborn globs of white foam cling to the corners of his mouth. ("Krashta twishnee mor pajirty Lazarus aiy tonikwi...")

Lazarus, a destitute who had once begged at the rich man's gate, had done one thing right in his life. The rich man hadn't. And now, clutching garbage as if it were gold, he sits under the crushing gavel of truth:

> He will punish those who do not know God and do not obey the gospel of our Lord Jesus. They will be punished with everlasting destruction and shut out from the presence of the Lord and from the majesty of his power.... (2 Thessalonians 1:8–9)

Was that the worst pain of all? For a man whose money had gained him entrance into most anyplace, for one whose influence had rarely failed to open doors, does it now kill him to know that he is shut out of the Presence where even that beggar Lazarus now resides?

*Doesn't he see the bridge?*

He shouts across the chasm as coherence visits briefly: "Lazarus, send someone back here. At least warn my relatives. Save them from this damnation!"

Rocking to and fro, he cuddles his possessions like a lover.

Momentarily, the dogs have moved on.

He glances over his shoulder to check for the lion.[4]

In a sense, the man in the three-piece rags can see. But in another sense, he can't. He can see well enough to swat flies. He can see to pick up assets such as cardboard and plastic and houses and investment accounts. But he can't *really* see. He can't see the lion's true identity. Can't see the source of his fear. Can't see the trash he collects for what it is. He can't see the bridge that leads to the Sanctuary, can't see that the door opens to everyone who knocks on it.

How did he and all those who sit in the pit with him acquire this degenerative problem of sight? I'll tell you. The lion, the Land of Wrath's lord, knows that his continuing rule depends on this endemic blindness. Hence his selfishly wicked strategy.

> And even if our gospel is veiled, it is veiled to those who are perishing. The god of this age has blinded the minds of unbelievers, so that they cannot see the light of the gospel of the glory of Christ, who is the image of God. (2 Corinthians 4:3–4)

We should not, however, give the lion too much credit. In every case he has a partner, a willing accomplice. The man in soiled pinstripes and everyone else in the mire have cooperated with the blindness. They can't see, but they don't mind the loss. Fact is, they've come to accept and even enjoy the darkness.

God doesn't respond joyously to this. He gives these people what they ask for:

> They perish because they refused to love the truth and so be saved. For this reason God sends them a powerful delusion so that they will believe the lie and so that all will be condemned who have not believed the truth but have delighted in wickedness. (2 Thessalonians 2:10–12)

It's a vicious cycle: fear of death, blindness, love of darkness, delusion, continuing to believe the lie, condemnation.

It's very dark. Very silent. All things considered, the pit holds no good reason to live.

## Two Legends

The blindness has reached epidemic proportions. We can observe it in two of the legends that are often told Outside.[5]

The first legend tells of a man who had two sons. The father went to the first son and said, "Son, go and work today in the vineyard."

"No, I don't want to," said the son, but later he changed his mind and went.

So the father went to the other son and said the same thing. The second son answered, "I will, sir," but he did not go.

When the two sons returned to the house at the end of the day, the father didn't really care who had actually gone into the vineyard. All he cared about was that his sons had good intentions. All that mattered to him, so the story goes, is that they sincerely meant well. So he rewarded the second son who had said he intended to go but didn't.

This story reminds the dwellers of darkness that the stupid prostitutes and tax collectors who had repented of their sinfulness and entered the Sanctuary had only fooled themselves. Obviously, they'll have to wait in line and go in after the more religious.

The second legend describes a landowner who planted a vineyard. He put a wall around it, dug a winepress in it, and built a watchtower. Then he rented the vineyard to some farmers and left on a journey. When the harvesttime approached, he sent his servants to the tenants to collect his fruit. The tenants seized his servants; they beat one, killed another, and stoned a third. Then he sent other servants to them, more than the first time, and the tenants treated them the same way. Last of all, he sent his son to them. "They will respect my son," he thought. (That statement always evokes a lot of laughter among Devastation's residents.)

But when the tenants saw the son, they said to each other, "This is the heir. Come, let's kill him and take his inheritance." So they threw him out of the vineyard and killed him.

The legend says that when the vineyard's owner returned, he saw the farmers' determination. He observed that nothing could stop them from keeping the vineyard, so he just decided to give it to them.

This is perhaps the Land of Wrath's most famous legend, for it reinforces the idea that God's kingdom belongs to those who insist on having it by their own means.

## The Final Scene

Let's end this horrific venture into the world Outside by looking into the future.

People have now come from east and west and north and south to take their places inside the Sanctuary at the feast of God's kingdom. Many of those "prostitutes" and "tax collectors" are there. They didn't have to wait in line after all. Indeed, the master of the Sanctuary welcomed them with a smile and a warm embrace.

But then some others who have known about the door for a long time have finally decided to cross the bridge and knock on the Sanctuary door. But the owner has closed and bolted the door. The rich man in designer rags has forsaken his trash so he can pound on the door. Together with the others who have finally made the journey, they stand outside knocking and pleading, "Sir, open the door for us!"

But the owner answers, "I don't know you or where you come from."

They cry out, "We ate and drank with you, and you taught in our streets. We saw your handiwork in the stars. We listened to your prophets and preachers. You whispered to our hearts."

But he replies, "I don't know you or where you come from. Away from me, all you evildoers!" [6]

Out of compassion, the owner of the Sanctuary has already warned us that the day will come when the door will no longer open. But some who have had adequate opportunity, who have passed up multiple chances to knock on the door, will ultimately delay too long and discover that to be "last" means to be left out.

## A Footnote for Skeptics

If you tend to doubt the reality of Devastation, I owe you an apology for watering down this subject. To be honest, my weak stomach held me back.

For your sake, I should have descended to another layer of reality, should have laid it on the line the way God does in His Word. But to do that, I would have had to address the subject of mouths full of cursing and bitterness. I don't excel at illustrating profanity, especially in a Christian book.

And I would have had to say that people outside the Sanctuary are in a hurry to shed blood. They like to kill people with knives or, if handier, words. Please accept my apology, but I'm not talented at describing gory scenes.

You can understand, therefore, why I also chickened out of describing the throats and tongues of people in the Land of Wrath. (I'm not making this up. You can read it yourself in Romans 3:9–18.) I didn't feel I could describe their throats as open graves. I've never seen an open grave in person. I've viewed many mass graves in documentaries of the Holocaust. I also have a friend who visited a church in Rwanda where hundreds of people had been slaughtered weeks before and left in a pile to rot. So based on what I've learned secondhand, I'd have to discuss rigor mortis, decaying skin, flies buzzing in wounds, sunken eye sockets, and the terrible stench. I couldn't handle that, but I admit it would have made a powerful statement about the corruption and deceit of people outside of Christ. I wouldn't have even needed to mention the viper poison gushing out the sides of their lips.

Besides, if your ears have been offended by words from the pit, you need no proof of the vileness of Devastation's residents. You already know how anger can crush a person's fragile self. You've seen profanity transform an amiable friend into a different and hard-to-love monster.

The ugliest description the Bible offers about the kingdom of Darkness, and the one I most wanted to avoid, is a seemingly innocent one. We've become so accustomed to seeing it every day that we have forgotten it is the most vile aspect of the kingdom of the roaring lion: "There is no fear of God before their eyes" (Romans 3:18). I don't write well enough to adequately portray this disaster. I sense it in my gut but can't put it into words; can't express the sad fact that many people lack the awareness that they need to revere God; can't communicate the tragedy that those orphaned people could have a Father who longs to adopt them.

So allow me to use calmer imagery. Let's return to Paul's letter to the Ephesians:

As for you, you were dead in your transgressions and sins, in which you used to live when you followed the ways of this world and of the ruler of the kingdom of the air, the spirit who is now at work in those who are disobedient. All of us also lived among them at one time, gratifying the cravings of our sinful nature and following its desires and thoughts. Like the rest, we were by nature objects of wrath. (Ephesians 2:1–3)

Not one of us needs tutoring in self-gratification. No parent ever says, "Let's see, we need to teach our little one how to tie shoes, feed himself, and be selfish."

Even if we escape unscathed by the lips-of-poison scenario, and if we can talk our way around the "dead in transgressions" part and dismiss as eccentric the bit about the "kingdom of the air," we *all* feel a jab from that last phrase: "We were by nature objects of wrath."

Maybe you're the person we'd all like to have as a roommate. You've never verbally abused anyone, and you have to really concentrate to think of anyone you hate. You avoided the excesses of youth, and rowdiness is not in your temperament analysis. But, just as the rest of us, you still face that nagging reality: Your very nature stinks. You're disciplined, self-controlled, and cordial. You're as winsome as a cool breeze under a palm tree. Your words bring sweetness to most situations. But your basic nature is rotten. If constraints were removed and witnesses turned the other way, given the right opportunity, you'd eventually pluck the forbidden fruit off the tree and take a nibble. Even if you never sinned a sin, your nature has already nabbed you in the net of condemnation.

And so many people are content to stay there. The most depressing aspect of life Outside is that people there don't want help even when Someone offers it to them. Thankfully there are exceptions, but most Wrathlings are happy right where they are. If Lazarus could have sent someone back to warn Pinstripe's brothers, they wouldn't have believed him, let alone heeded his words.

*O*nce I watched a deceased princess ride through town in a hearse. The streets were lined with throngs of mourners throwing flowers lovingly toward her black motorcade, a final tribute to the one they loved so dearly. In life she had done so much good for so many unfortunate and downcast people, and as a result, had won the affection of millions.

As I watched the somber procession, with her lifeless body encased in a coffin draped with a flag and flowers, my mind surmised where the princess—the soul of her—had gone. From what vantage point did she view the proceedings? And I wondered what would transpire if, for only a moment or two, the princess could revisit her body, raise the lid on that adorned coffin, and sit up. The escorts would stop in their tracks, the hearse would come to a halt, the camera would zoom in to see the nature of this phenomenon, the announcer would query the impossible event, and a sizable portion of the human race would stare transfixed at their television screens, breathless.

Of course, I don't know what the princess would say in such a case, for I am not God, and I don't know the condition of her relationship with the Savior. But I believe I can unequivocally state that she would tell the world of a great chasm fixed between those on the Outside and those inside the Sanctuary. She would warn her admirers to do whatever they could to avoid the Land of Wrath and its torment. She would tell them to repent. She would tell *us* to repent.

I'm convinced her appeal would be an impassioned one. The princess would feel more deeply about this short message than she had about any of the other causes she had fought for while on earth. And after she had given her plea, after the coffin had once again closed over her lifeless body, after the procession had made its way out of camera sight, and after the day of the funeral yielded to weeks and months of normalcy, most of those who stood mesmerized before their televisions that day would recall the event and remember with pleasantness the princess's kindness, even in death, to communicate a message of love. They would think of how surreal the plea had been, how much the princess seemed to have changed so quickly, and how they preferred to remember her as she had been in life rather than the way she had become in death. In effect, the plea of the princess would go unheeded. In the end, people would not be convinced—even if someone rose from the dead to tell them.

*God, my words are few. My heart is sickened by what I see.*

*I'm prone to argue, prone to protest.*

*To think that so many people endure this foul state . . .*

*There is no greater tragedy.*

# CHAPTER FIVE

# But God
# Roars Louder

*She touched the wood with her toe.*
*"Daddy, how long has this bridge been here?"*
*"For a long time, my child."*
*"Is it safe to walk on?"*
*"I'm not sure."*
*"It seems strong enough."*
*"Maybe, but it's risky."*
*"Daddy, it's shaped like a cross."*
*"Mmm."*
*"Look, it can hold me!"*

One day, God's patience snapped. It began as a clap of thunder in the distance. His discontent rumbled over the hills of villainy, sending forth the first warning shots that His silence would soon cease.

The ocean began to swell, turning the deep green water into white foam, reflecting the Almighty's building fury. The winds picked up the tempo as they began to howl, building into gale force, breaking into the bellowing roar of divine indignation. God was fed up with the captivity of souls, sick and tired of the despicable prince's pompous rule.

The roofs and shutters of the Land of Wrath lost their grip and sailed uncontrollably into the wind, exposing dismal hovels of fear. Then the earth began to shake, and the foundations of the mountains trembled, shaking with God's burning rage.

Smoke rose from His nostrils and consuming fire burst forth from His mouth. He split the heavens because the perishing cried out; He came to rescue those entangled in the snares of death. From His Sanctuary, He heard their wail of distress.

So He mounted the cherubim and soared on the wings of the wind. He made darkness His hiding place, the sky's dark rain clouds His canopy. Out of the brightness of His presence, the clouds advanced over the dreary land, hailstones and bolts of lightning emissaries of the infuriated King. The Lord thundered from heaven, the voice of the Most High roared. He shot His arrows into the lewd oppression and scattered the devilish minions in a thousand directions. He threw great bolts of lightning and routed the hierarchy of hate. The valleys of the sea were exposed, and the foundations of the earth laid bare at the Lord's rebuke, at the blast of breath from His nostrils.[1]

Yes, the God of love could bear the sight no longer. He could no longer endure the pain. He had to rescue the people brought forth from His yearning arms, the family He created for holiness.

And so He rose that day in vindication so righteous as to be virtuous. He rose against the devastation and waste. He rose in disgust at the culture of filth, His blood running hot with rage over the crippling depravity. He rose to crush the skull of the vile rebel who had deceived His creation, and with flaming eyes and fuming anger, with clenched fists raised toward heaven, with holy sandals planted squarely on the sludge of deception's kingdom, God lifted His thunderous voice and shook the rafters of rottenness. His glaring eyes pierced right through the lion, and with words sharpened like a saber, God challenged His enemy to the duel of the ages: "Meet me at Golgotha!"

## The Warrior

The challenge given, it now remained for God to select His warrior. He didn't have a difficult choice, for only one was fit for the fight. To send Him was a costly sacrifice, but God had to do it. So great was their love for the hopeless ones that the Father and the Warrior didn't hesitate.

For centuries, they had known the requirement. Only the timing needed to be revealed. And when the time came, the Warrior who held all our hope was ready.

Jesus Himself gave an early glimmer of the approaching duel. He was in

His hometown and the locals were on hand. In the synagogue, Jesus rolled open the crackling parchment, patiently finding the particular spot in the Book of Isaiah. The passage unfurled, He revealed the nature of His appointment:

"The Spirit of the Lord is on me,
    because he has anointed me to preach good news to the poor.
He has sent me to proclaim freedom for the prisoners
    and recovery of sight for the blind,
to release the oppressed,
    to proclaim the year of the Lord's favor." (Luke 4:18–19)

Have you ever been enraged at injustice—not just angry but absolutely infuriated? If so, then you know it's the most gripping emotion humans can experience. Nothing stirs up the bowels of passion, nothing sets the teeth ajar, nothing furls the lips and ignites the mind more than righteous indignation.

But feeling and even expressing the sensations of wrath do not dismantle injustice. Unbridled ire only fuels evil fire. Instead, one needs a wise and controlled plan of action that can unravel the cords of wrong.

God is very wise.

And so He was ready with a plan. It called for sneaking into enemy territory and releasing the hostages. It held back no resource, reserved no secret weapon. The plan was completely committed to success, even at the cost of human life.

The strategy used the unlikely scenario of a baby born out of wedlock to refugee parents. It involved a man telling a skeptical congregation in Nazareth that He was the guerrilla soldier who would release Devastation's captives, the healer who would mend broken hearts. The strategy entailed keeping an appointment on a hill known for shame.

The plan went by a common name given uncommon meaning. It was called "redemption."

## Back to Song!

There's a proverb that says, "The name of the LORD is a strong tower; the righteous run to it and are safe" (Proverbs 18:10). That's how I feel after writing the previous chapter. I actually became nauseated at some points as I described Devastation. I kept thinking, *I must return to the Sanctuary! Let's finish this chapter once and for all!*

And now, finally, we're here in Christ, right where we belong. The music of Sanctuary worship has replaced the Land of Wrath's crippling wails of anguish. Truth's light has overcome deception's darkness; the fragrance of praise has scattered sin's stench. Here, meaning has replaced purposelessness. Rejoice! There's a reason to live, a Person to worship, an alternative to fright. Join in the incredible joy of the Sanctuary hymn: "In him we have redemption through his blood, the forgiveness of sins, in accordance with the riches of God's grace that he lavished on us with all wisdom and understanding" (Ephesians 1:7–8).

I glory in repeating that *in Him* we have everything we need, including deliverance from the Land of Wrath and the devouring lion that prowls it. *Redemption* is defined as a "setting free by payment of a ransom."[2] While it has a future and ultimate aspect, Sanctuary praise tells us Jesus has *already* set free His believers ("we have redemption")! Christ has legitimately purchased our freedom. Redemption belongs in the Sanctuary treasure chest; it belongs to you, an ornament for your wall, a part of your dowry.

Don't let your feelings and struggles deprive you of this reality: Christ has set you free from the bondage of sin. He has rescued you from Devastation. He has delivered you from fear of the lion.

How? By paying the purchase price in full. God had demanded the release of His beloved children. He had chosen and adopted them, and now He wanted them back from the Land of Wrath. And so Jesus Christ went to Golgotha to settle the score, to destroy the devil's works (1 John 3:8).

Our Warrior went to Golgotha with a surprising battle plan. He knew that true victory could come only through apparent defeat. He needed to die so we could live. He wouldn't fight by dealing out blows to helmets and armor; instead, He would battle by receiving stabs to His skin and soul. He went to Golgotha not to unleash vengeance, but to satisfy justice.

The payment? His life. And as His lifeblood drained from His body, the currency of ransom was counted on the table of justice. As the blood flowed down His legs and dripped from His toes onto the rock below, two events transpired. One, His physical life gradually left Him. Two, the right to live eternally was given to all of His own. He bought us back, one drop at a time, until we were fully free.

Humankind has witnessed the payment of exorbitant prices throughout history. People and corporations have pushed millions of dollars across desks in New York and Paris for paintings or racehorses or other prizes. But on a certain Friday in Jerusalem, history's largest purchase price was paid. We were bought with the precious blood of God's sole Son.

To what shall we liken it? To a whole nation sending into battle an army of one, having no other way to fight save that solitary soldier. Imagine that that one is *your* only and beloved son. Imagine trudging through the mist onto the battlefield to honor *your* dead with *your* tears.

In other words, the price was inestimable.

But so was the prize. The plan called redemption worked perfectly, for it restored to God all He had ever wanted.

## The Greater of Two Hills

So much happened when Christ died for our sins—not just on earth but in heaven. Could we stretch our minds to encompass some of that higher drama? To do so, return with me to Jerusalem, and imagine the story that two of that great city's hills—Mount Moriah and Golgotha—could tell.

Mount Moriah was a grand and regal hill, boasting a star-studded history. How many mountains could brag about Abraham's raised knife and his son's quiet faith? Now the mount proudly wore the magnificent temple that Herod built. The pearl of the City of David, the center of Israel's faith, jutted toward the sky in gleaming splendor. Now its priests busily prepared for the Passover celebrations.

Probably just three thousand feet away stood Moriah's diminutive half-brother, Golgotha. Golgotha didn't even count as one of Jerusalem's seven hills. By appearance, it was plain. By history, it was despicable. But by destiny, it was about to become glorious.

For you see, while the priests scurried about the temple on Moriah, preparing to enter the Holy Place, Golgotha was about to host the High Priest of heaven. With sandaled feet, the Rock of Ages was scheduled to walk onto the rock of shame and step into the eternal Holy of Holies, into the temple of the Living God.

In Herod's temple, the priests had become quite adept at offering a day's worth of oblations without soiling their garments with goat's blood. In a moment, on the hill of ignominy, the eternal High Priest would come to perform His sole task: to spill His own blood shamelessly onto Himself and wherever else it would happen to fall.

The two hills could not have been more different. By all appearances, Mount Moriah for its temple was clearly glorious and admirable. But no one would want to visit the ugly hill of Golgotha.

Isaiah the prophet knew how unsightly a place Golgotha would be. He foretold how disfigured the High Priest would become on that hill. The ancient prophet knew that the Messiah would be mauled, displaying neither beauty nor majesty. Instead, He'd be despised and rejected by men. Man of sorrows. Familiar with suffering. Like one from whom men hide their faces. Stricken. Smitten. Pierced. Crushed. Oppressed and afflicted. Led like a lamb to the slaughter.[3]

But Isaiah also knew there was a purpose for all the ugliness. Jesus would take up our infirmities. Carry our sorrows. Be pierced for our transgressions. Crushed for our iniquities. The punishment that brought us peace was upon Him. By His wounds we are healed. The Lord has laid on Him the iniquity of us all.

That's why Moriah, the regal mount, deferred to Golgotha that day. Call it a passing of the baton. Think of it as a recognition of greatness.

The shadow bowed to the substance. The copy yielded to the original. The earthly acquiesced to the heavenly. The temple applauded the Sanctuary.

The worship on Moriah grew dim in the spiritual realm that day, lessened by the increasing brilliance that shone on the Redeemer. Perhaps, like John the Baptist, who had said, "He must increase but I must decrease," the Temple tipped its hat to the heavenly High Priest on the hill called Skull. And maybe the Sanctuary saluted back to the stone and bronze, acknowledging a job well done, releasing it from its duty and accepting the immense responsibility on Himself.

Though no mortal noticed it, heaven's eyes could see that the golden lamp-stand beamed a smile over the wall to the Light of the World. The table of showbread turned over duties to the Bread of Life. The golden altar of incense giggled with delight at the fragrant offering ascending over Golgotha. The Ark of the Covenant sighed deeply with relief that the new covenant of the heart had finally come. And the cherubim who covered the mercy seat joyfully fluttered their golden wings at the deluge of grace raining down and washing away condemnation.

Caiaphas, the high priest on Mount Moriah, didn't have eyes to see this phenomenal display. He had missed his true calling. What should have been the grand climax of glorious centuries of preparation turned out a dismal failure of perception. So thick were the blindfolds that the high priest didn't know that his heavenly counterpart, the true High Priest, was even now within the Holy of heavenly Holies, offering once and for all the sacrifice for all of humankind's sin.

But the High Priest of the new covenant didn't require the acknowledgment of the Old. The new Mediator bridged the gap single-handedly.

Job well done, O bulls and goats of the sacrifice! You pictured Him well. You pointed the way.

O you tender lambs of the ages, you who gave your lifeblood helplessly. Look, see Him there, the fulfillment of your prophecies. The Lamb of God takes away the sin of the world![4]

## Uncondemned

We can only bear Christ's disfigurement in light of the value of what it produced: "the forgiveness of sins" (Ephesians 1:7).

But what is forgiveness? Some inadequate synonyms for it are *condone, overlook, disregard.* Equally weak substitutes are *make allowances for, let off the hook,* and *bury the hatchet.* If we still lived under the old covenant, these words might suffice for the forgiveness we experience when worshiping at Herod's temple.

But you and I are under the new covenant. Forget the sedan; we're driving the sports car! We can't settle for anything less than high-powered synonyms for forgiveness: *pardon, acquit, exonerate.* Or how about *remove guilt, cancel, void, delete, erase, clear the books, wipe the slate clean?*

In the second hymn of the Sanctuary, the word translated *forgiveness* (*aphesis,* in Ephesians 1:7) connotes the idea of a "letting go" or "dismissal." This same word once applied to horse racing; the starting post was called the *aphesis* because that's where horses were released to run a race.[5] Interesting picture, isn't it? Jesus went up to Golgotha and told our sins to take a hike, to flee like horses from the starting gate!

If you don't believe me, let's return to that Nazarene synogogue where Jesus told the hometown folks that He had a bigger destiny than making furniture. Remember what He said? "He has sent me to proclaim freedom [that is, *aphesis*] for the prisoners...to release [that is, to provide *aphesis* for] the oppressed" (Luke 4:18).

The reason for all the horrible Messiah-bashing that Isaiah the prophet foresaw—and the hub of Sanctuary praise—is that Jesus Christ ultimately and permanently bought a way for us to leave Devastation. He extended a helping hand to those in the mire of lostness. His cross formed a reliable bridge into eternal life.

And for those who accept His offer and enter His Sanctuary, there awaits the most incredible sensation possible. When we enter into Christ, then and only then do we find real forgiveness, true release from sin and guilt. Fathom this: "Therefore, there is now *no condemnation* for those who are in Christ Jesus" (Romans 8:1, emphasis mine).

There's a place where you don't have to hide. You don't have to dread someone discovering your faults, don't have to fear someone itemizing your sins. In Christ, the Sanctuary of the believer, there is *no* condemnation. There, you are accepted totally and completely, right now. And I mean right now, which is another way of saying just as you are, shortcomings galore. Every sin that you commit can't even begin to threaten your sure standing in Christ. Remember, He draws from a deep well of grace: "in accordance with the riches of God's grace that he lavished on us with all wisdom and understanding" (Ephesians 1:7–8).

If we could just begin to appropriate this incredible truth into our daily existence, we would be revolutionized. Our lives would be filled with joy, freedom, and purpose instead of anxiety, guilt, and depression. Our families would change. We might not even recognize our churches! The lack of condemnation in Christ's body is, to me, the most overpowering force of Sanctuary living. It is also the least experienced. Total acceptance before God is our legitimate birthright, but we live as if God and everyone else constantly condemns us!

Remember the soldiers on Golgotha who robbed Christ? Remember the scribes and Pharisees who had just framed Him? Even of them Jesus prayed, "Father, forgive them, for they do not know what they are doing" (Luke 23:34). Father, release their sin, send it away like a horse out of the starting gate.

Why can't we grasp the reality of forgiveness? Why do we talk about it and preach about it, yet live under a fog of guilt and condemnation? A. W. Tozer exhorts us in this regard:

> We must believe that God's mercy is boundless, free, and, through Jesus Christ our Lord, available to us now in our present situation. We may plead for mercy for a lifetime in unbelief, and at the end of our days be still no more than sadly hopeful that we shall somewhere, sometime, receive it. This is to starve to death just outside the banquet hall into which we have been warmly invited. Or we may, if we will, lay hold on the mercy of God by faith, enter the hall, and sit down with the bold and avid souls who will not allow diffidence and unbelief to keep them from the feast of fat things prepared for them.[6]

Excuse my bluntness, but in the Sanctuary you can be your crummy self. You need not perform there. (You've entered because of *His* performance, not yours.) God intends that His Sanctuary be filled with crummy people who have received complete acceptance from Christ and from one another.

When Jesus read His job description from the scroll of Isaiah, He said He had come to "release the oppressed" (Luke 4:18). But the word *oppressed* doesn't fully communicate Jesus' meaning. A fuller translation is "I came to release those who have been broken in pieces."[7] Jesus knew that He had come to put broken people back together.

And He knows that *you* are broken. In fact, He may see the cracks and scattered pieces better than you do! He knows your hurts and depression. And so He went up to Golgotha, not for you *alone* but, as only God can, for you *especially.* Jesus died for the whole world *one life at a time.*

## One Life at a Time

Do you recall the woman doubled over in the Land of Wrath? Luke, a medical doctor who had a holistic view of diagnostics, described her as a woman "who had been crippled by a spirit for eighteen years" (Luke 13:11). Now witness what the Redeemer had in mind for her...

The Lion of Judah was in the synagogue one day. There He saw a doubled-over woman hiding along the wall. Her drooping hair shielded her face. Well-acquainted with the ground, she spent only a portion of her strength looking up, including at Him.

He looked at her and saw right to her very core. He discerned the forgotten hopes and heard the cruel criticisms. He recognized her husband's abandonment and her children's embarrassment.

What He saw made Him angry, not at the woman but at the creature that *really* deserved to stoop toward the dust, the stalking lion whose treachery had undermined this woman and her family.

Jesus knew what He wanted to do. But today was the Sabbath, the day hallowed by proud legalists. If He healed the debilitated woman today, He would never hear the end of it.

So Jesus concluded that it was a *perfect* day for a miracle—a day to grind legalism into the ground.

He called the woman to Himself. Does that seem cruel? Couldn't He have much more easily breached the distance between them? I may be reading into the story—forgive me if I am—but doesn't it seem that Jesus made it a habit to call people to Himself, allowing them—allowing this woman—a moment in the sun? And didn't His calling allow her to make a declaration to the throngs repulsed for years by her indignity, letting her say with each shuffling step, "I have been bound, but You can untie me"?

When He called her, she came, doubled over with pain. Jesus said to her,

"Woman, you are set free from your infirmity."

To complete the drama, Jesus extended His hands and rested them upon her. (This required that He stoop down.) She immediately stood up straight.

At this point, Luke, the sole recorder of this event, displays the gift of understatement he had honed through years in the medical field. He simply says that, after straightening up, the woman "praised God."

I'll bet she did! I imagine she praised God as she looked Him right in the eyes! How fitting that the first one she should look upon with restored dignity would be her Healer and Redeemer.

Then, perhaps, she brushed back her hair from her face and looked forgivingly into the faces of her scoffers. I doubt if any sight in this world could compare with the sheer glamour of her first smile in years.

And I can just bet that the lesser lion squealed off the scene with tail tucked, taking his chattering minions with him. For as Jesus touched her, the force of redemption had dislodged them from their home. Self-pity, resentment, suicide, hatred…all evicted after a perfectly good eighteen-year tenancy!

I suppose the lady couldn't wait to go home. I can't help wondering what the kids would say when, arriving home from school, they saw their mother dusting the *top* of the cabinet! And her husband must have swallowed hard a few times, especially seeing her looking beautiful in that outfit he'd bought her twenty years before.

The touch of redemption made the crooked straight.

Still does. Chances are you're not literally, physically bent over, but your life has probably gone crooked in a few places. In what ways have you become bent? Do you find yourself powerless to overcome a perpetual sin? Has your private world become poisoned by bitterness? Is your body diseased? Does your soul seem terminally ill?

The Sanctuary door is wide open. Within, Jesus still says, "Beloved, you are set free from your infirmity."

## Strange Dreams

Now that Christ has won the victory on Golgotha, God is full swing into a publicity campaign. The Good News is out! He will go to any length to bring the joy of redemption wherever it's welcome. And the light is overcoming some shadowy corners.

Those who have dedicated their lives to bringing the gospel to Islamic countries tell us that a high percentage of Muslims who convert to Jesus Christ do so as a result of a supernatural dream or vision. I recently read that the Good News reaches about one-third of Turkish converts in this way. This phenomenon might stretch our theological comfort zone, but how can we raise an eyebrow when God is using a centuries-old method of revelation to bring truth into lands where Christianity is forbidden? In a country where a preacher would be killed, a Bible burned, a church disbanded, and a livelihood cut off for the gospel's sake, how perfectly appropriate for the hidden hope of Golgotha to reveal Himself in a person's dream!

Jesus Christ seems to be visiting many beloved Muslim friends each year during the holy month of Ramadan. During that month in 1991, a young Muslim man on Kalimantan (formerly Borneo) had a disturbing dream. In this dream, he was sitting with his arms tied to the arms of a chair. A man he recognized as Jesus approached him. Jesus touched the ropes, and they fell from the man's arms. Then Jesus said, "Look for the pole." Puzzled, the man asked Jesus, "What pole?" Jesus simply repeated, "Look for the pole."

The young man woke from his dream wondering about its meaning. He tried to decipher it but couldn't. After a few days, he simply forgot about it.

Two years later, during Ramadan in 1993, the same young man had another dream. Once again, Jesus appeared to him. "I told you to look for the pole," Jesus said. "Why haven't you done what I asked?" In his dream, the Muslim asked Jesus, "Where is this pole and how can I find it?" Jesus pointed to a distant hill. "Go look for the pole." The young man ran and ran in the direction Jesus had pointed. For what seemed like miles, he rushed through thornbushes and dense jungle. Exhausted, he finally came to a clearing, and there before him stood a cross. This was the pole Jesus had told him to search for!

The next day, the young Muslim went to the mosque leader and told him about the strange dreams, asking if the imam knew the meaning of the dreams and of the cross. The imam replied, "Search for the truth." The eager man pressed on: "Is the Christian Jesus the truth then?" The imam merely replied, "Search for the truth."

The next night, the young man had yet another dream. In this dream he saw a cemetery that he recognized as a Christian graveyard because all the graves had crosses at their heads. Suddenly all the graves opened, the buried rose into the sky, and Jesus greeted them. The young Muslim cried to Jesus, saying he wasn't ready because he didn't yet have the cross!

The man awoke very disturbed. How could he discover this cross for himself? He knew of a small church near his village and traveled there to find the pastor. He told the pastor about his dreams and asked for help in understanding them. The pastor explained the dreams' meanings and showed him the verse where Jesus said, "I am the way and the truth and the life. No one comes to the Father except through me" (John 14:6). The young man began attending that church, and after a few weeks, he gave his life to the Lord Jesus Christ.[8]

*J*esus eagerly beckons timid ones to the cross that rescues them from Devastation. One by one, they're venturing into the Sanctuary. One by one, they're coming home.

I'd be derelict in my duties if I didn't ask you this question: have you come to the pole? Christ went there with you in mind, went down in battle for your deliverance. There's one way you can bring honor to His death. Embrace and accept His payment for you. Come on home.[9]

*God, if I ever sound ungrateful (and I know I do),*

*would You please put my ingratitude in the stupidity file?*

*The push-and-shove world can easily knock my perspective off center.*

*But right now,*

*I'm seeing more clearly. I'm seeing my Warrior go to battle for me.*

I'm seeing Him take the ultimate hit.

I'm seeing my Sanctuary ascending Golgotha and

kicking the tar out of Devastation.

I'm seeing my self-condemnation race off into the sunset

on the speeding stallion called forgiveness.

I'm seeing the cords of sin unraveling at my feet.

I'm feeling the sensation of gradually standing erect.

And I'm seeing that the essence of life is as simple as finding

the clearing and bowing before the pole of the Savior.

And so, perspective intact for the moment, I am at rest.

I feel accepted, crummy as I am.

And I am profoundly grateful.

# It'll All Add Up Just Fine

*God always pulls off His plans on time, and right now*
*He wants us to continue waiting.*

When you and I read the story of Golgotha, we have the benefit of hindsight. We know that Jesus remained firm till the end. We know He rose from the dead. We know that His disciples eventually proved faithful and that the largest religious movement in the history of humankind sprang forth from God's working in those brave men, a movement that continues to this day. In short, we know the story has a happy ending.

But for a moment, put some blinders on your hindsight and place yourself at the foot of the cross, convinced that this was the end. Convinced Jesus had performed His last miracle, told His last parable, given His last assurance. If there was any hope on that hill, it was well hidden as Jesus hung there.

Peter, his walk on the water now a distant recollection, warmed his hands by the fire, trying to blend in. *Well, it was good while it lasted—I'll have to say that. But it's back to the sea for me. I'll still share His teachings with the folks back home, still try to convince my relatives to follow Jesus. But it will be mighty difficult with Him gone. Mighty difficult.*

John was another one who must have thought the future looked bleak. The "Son of Thunder" wasn't roaring now. Tough and tender John, whose mother had envisioned a heavenly entitlement for her sons at the Savior's right and left hands, was now left clutching for air. *We had such great plans. The kingdom would grow so big and help so many. But what now? He said He had to leave, that He would return. But surely this isn't what He meant. Surely His plans have gone awry.*

But let's now turn our attention, again without hindsight, to the one who knelt beneath the cross and perhaps hurt the deepest. Consider the one who couldn't find a comfortable position with the granite pressing on her knees and the sword piercing her soul. The others dealt with dashed hopes; they stung with disappointment as confused friends. But this woman was there from the very beginning. She was the first to know of His coming, the first to know the hope. It was her heart that pondered His calling, her pain that brought Him forth into the world, her breasts that nurtured His frail life. And now, clutching loose stones in agonized fists, she resisted with all her might the temptation to give in to despair.

*Chosen of God…Ha!* she could have thought. *This can't be where it was supposed to lead. All these years of raising this child and waiting for His kingdom, only to have His life cut short like this! I fail to see God's favor in a shameful death.*

Mary hurt as only a mother can. Her calendar didn't have a tomorrow. Beyond the stony real estate that stood between her and her dying Son, she couldn't see or think of anything. All was blackness. All was loss. It was over.

The future still has the habit of dropping out of sight. All of us have had times when our future seemed to explode into a million bits, never to be recovered. Maybe you can still hear the blast ringing in your ears. A future can detonate in plenty of ways: the loss of a scholarship, job offer, or promotion; a divorce, a spouse's death, a broken engagement; a child's rebellion or a parent's affair; a child's death or the onset of terminal disease; a house fire, a break-in, a mugging; enduring abuse or the memory of abuse; a miscarriage or stillbirth; an auto accident or the "crash" of a ministry.

Sometimes a future doesn't explode; it just leaves unannounced. This may be the hardest to cope with, for you can't point to a tragedy and say, "I had a future until that creep divorced me." No explanation to offer sense or comfort or an object for anger. Just the hollow absence of hope, the deafening silence of any expectation. Depression can create such a silence, as can spiritual dryness.

A proverb of the Luo tribe in western Kenya says, "You snatched us from the jaws of the lion but you dropped us among the hyenas." Though our heads tell us God wouldn't do such a thing, our hearts sometimes feel as if He has.

I reckon Mary felt that way when she followed her beloved Son to Golgotha.

And I reckon Jesus knew it. In fact, I know He did. He had a future for His mother, just as He has a future for you and me. He's a Man with the ultimate, overarching plan, and He doesn't lose the details in the magnificence of it.

Take Mary's case. Jesus looked down from His elevated agony and saw her among the other women. I don't even have to tell you which disciple recorded what happened: "When Jesus saw his mother there, and the disciple whom he loved standing nearby, he said to his mother, 'Dear woman, here is your son,' and to the disciple, 'Here is your mother.' From that time on, this disciple took her into his home" (John 19:26–27). Jesus cared about His mother's disillusionment, and so He entrusted her to John's family. There she would have provision, spiritual encouragement, and a future.

But how can we, living centuries after that afternoon near Jerusalem, know the same sense of our Master's concern? How can we feel Jesus' empathy when we have no hope?

Of course we can read our Bibles and understand His plans for us. We can reflect with comfort on His words, "In my Father's house are many rooms; if it were not so, I would have told you. I am going there to prepare a place for you" (John 14:2). But Jesus wants to give us more than His promises. He wants the promises to come with the reality of His presence. So He made a quiet but revolutionary announcement before He died. Watch this carefully:

> And I will ask the Father, and he will give you another Counselor to be with you forever—the Spirit of truth. The world cannot accept him, because it neither sees him nor knows him. But you know him, for he lives with you and will be in you. *I will not leave you as orphans; I will come to you.* Before long, the world will not see me anymore, but you will see me. Because I live, you also will live. On that day you will realize that I am in my Father, and *you are in me, and I am in you.* (John 14:16–20, emphasis mine)

Do you know why He didn't leave us as orphans? Because the Father has adopted us. And do you know how He planned to give us assurance all of our lives about our bright future? By giving us His own life—by living in us and letting us live in Him. In short, by providing Himself as our Sanctuary.

Have you ever entered a calm house, one where serenity permeates every room? What is the cause for such peace? Maybe you think it's because the house has no teenagers or toddlers! But that's not it. There's a different reason.

Perhaps you'd say it's because of peaceful surroundings: soft sofas, pleasing plants, soothing sunlight, some relaxing music, or a fragrant aroma coming from the kitchen. But are these surroundings the *cause* of the peacefulness or the *effect* of it? Don't you usually find that behind external serenity is a serene home-maker? Isn't the source of a calm home a host at peace? (You can tell what I think.)

That's the way it is in the Sanctuary. When we experience the reality of life in Christ, anxiety has no hook to hang its hat on. There's no welcome mat for stress. And you know why, don't you? The Homemaker has established serenity within, and it permeates the heart of every guest. It's difficult to worry in the presence of the One who has everything under control. His plan holds a good future for each and every one of us. His peace covers every circumstance. And that peace is ours if we are soaking up the calmness of His life.

May I call upon your imagination once again? Some reassuring music now courses through the Sanctuary, a hymn telling of Jesus' steady hand on the future:

> And he made known to us the mystery of his will according to his good pleasure, which he purposed in Christ, to be put into effect when the times will have reached their fulfillment—to bring all things in heaven and on earth together under one head, even Christ. In him we were also chosen, having been predestined according to the plan of him who works out everything in conformity with the purpose of his will, in order that we, who were the first to hope in Christ, might be for the praise of his glory. (Ephesians 1:9–12)

The plan called redemption didn't end at Golgotha. In fact, the future was never so bright as on that apparently dark day. Jesus didn't just deliver *from* Devastation. He also delivered *to* a final destination.

## Mystery No More

Listen more closely to the hymn. Let's not miss its assurances.

First, *God has shared with us the secret of the ages.* He has brought us into His confidence and "made known to us the mystery of his will." The mouths of prophets watered to know what we can know. The necks of the angels crane to see what we can see. Yet the Father has taken delight—He has indulged His "good pleasure"—to show us more than previously known! What is the mystery? The apostle Paul sums it up in his personal mission statement:

> I have become its servant by the commission God gave me to present to you the word of God in its fullness—*the mystery that has been kept hidden for ages and generations, but is now disclosed to the saints. To them God has chosen to make known among the Gentiles the glorious riches of this mystery, which is Christ in you, the hope of glory.* (Colossians 1:25–27, emphasis mine)

I find it encouraging that many people of Jewish descent now know Christ as their Savior, for God has historically called them His chosen ones. These Messianic Jews have discovered the mystery kept under wraps from generations of their forebears. You can almost hear the consternation that must have coursed through those ancestors' minds:

- "If God is for the Jews, why does our Old Testament talk so much about the Gentiles?"
- "If the Messiah is going to restore Israel, why are things going so poorly for us?"
- "If Jesus is the Messiah, why doesn't he overthrow the Romans?"

In other words, *"What in the world is God doing?"*

Though Golgotha seemed a failure to most, there God exposed the mysteries that He had kept shrouded for centuries. He revealed that:

- His heart was for the Jews, yes, but His love was too big to exclude Gentiles.
- He had bigger dreams than restoring Israel; He wanted to redeem a holy nation of all peoples.
- He wouldn't establish a political kingdom with Jerusalem as world capital but a spiritual kingdom centered in the Sanctuary of His Son.

I don't know about you, but when someone shares with me something deeply personal, I'm honored. I take it as a trust to guard carefully. So I find it mind-boggling that God has entrusted a long-kept secret with us. He has pulled us aside and honored us with the news that His Son is the hope for all the earth.

The second assurance of the hymn is this: *God knows how much time will pass before He wraps up history.* Do you ever wonder if God is still watching the clock? Ever think that He really paid attention to time those first hundred or so years after Christ, but then became casual about keeping a schedule?

Let me illustrate with a true story. You probably know that in many parts of the world people don't obsess over promptness as do folks in North America or Europe. Africa, where Lyn and I serve as missionaries, is one of those places. In fact, we often joke that if you're on "African time," the important thing isn't to arrive at the appointed hour but to have a good time once you do. Well, one time a missionary took a Kenyan pastor from Nairobi to the Mombasa coast to see his relatives. After arriving in town, the missionary and pastor decided they would drive back to Nairobi the next day. Since the two were spending the night in different neighborhoods, they agreed to meet at nine o'clock the next morning at a prearranged place.

The next morning, the missionary went to pick up the pastor, and wouldn't you know it, he had car trouble. Major car trouble. It took the whole day to fix the car. The missionary was distraught, for he had no way to contact the pastor about the delay. So he fretted and fussed. Finally, near dark, the car was fixed. The next morning (now a whole day late) the missionary woke up early and rushed to the appointed meeting spot, hoping he could find his pastor friend.

When the missionary arrived, he was pleasantly shocked to see the pastor standing calmly and happily right where they had agreed to meet. The missionary apologized profusely, explaining the entire ordeal of his car problems. The African pastor couldn't quite understand the missionary's agitation. "Don't be upset. You're not *that* late. I've only been waiting here for fifteen minutes!"[1]

I wonder if God is partial to African time. God is not late; He just isn't bound by our timetables. Fact is, God always pulls off His plans right on time, and right now He wants us to continue waiting. When will He intervene? "When the times will have reached their fulfillment" (Ephesians 1:10).

A first-century Greek speaker would have used the word *fulfillment*[2] to describe an auditorium full of sound or a garden full of scents. A Greek accountant would have used it to tell a client that his account was paid up. A ship's captain would have shouted this word when the last bundle of cargo was thrown into the hold: "It's full! There's no more room." In the same way, God watches the progress of His endeavor, and when the time is just right He'll say, "That's it. Time's up!"

When that time comes, what will God do? Our hymn's third assurance provides the incredible answer: *God will sum up everything in His Son.* Now we're getting somewhere! The "mystery"—the unveiling to us of God's amazing plan to gather a new people in Christ consisting of both Jews and Gentiles—is leading to a historic climax in the fullness of time. And why? For something worth a million-year wait. Impatience, take a vacation! God will "bring all things in heaven and on earth together under one head, even Christ" (Ephesians 1:10). Imagine that!

This is no part-time endeavor, no trial business venture. This is the divine Entrepeneur going for all the marbles! God intends a culmination involving no less than "all things in heaven and on earth"! That leaves nothing out. And He plans to bring these all together "under one head,"[3] our Lord and Savior Jesus Christ.

At the time God chooses, all the parts and pieces of heaven and earth will come together like a huge puzzle. All the random factors of human history will be totaled up, and the sum will be Jesus Christ. All the questions of the ages will be asked yet again, and the answer to them all will be the Son of God. The Father will orchestrate the finale of time itself, and the symphony's theme will be the Savior.

Who else but the Lord of all could embrace both heaven and earth? What else but the Sanctuary could encompass both? I can't fathom how He will do it, how He will expose every wrong and punish every injustice. I don't know how God will judge yet remain gracious toward the Christian who embezzled, the pastor who wronged his congregation, or the believer who abused his daughters, but I know He will. I know we will witness His judgments and say, "That's fair. That's just the right thing to do."

And who can imagine what it will be like when Hinduism and Buddhism and Islam and all their brothers finally admit that the weakened frame that went to Golgotha was the Way, the Truth, and the Life after all? One can only dream of the day when world banking institutions and the world's most powerful fraternities will release their fistfuls of money and bow in realization that the only investment of lasting value is faith in a poor Galilean!

You see, the hymn in the Sanctuary doesn't call us to decipher whether this summation of heaven and earth in Christ refers to the church age or the millennial kingdom or the eternal state. I don't think God's heart will skip a beat if we cannot agree on the timing of the Rapture. Look around you. Behold the ever-growing population in the Sanctuary. See them coming, entering into the joy of life in Christ. Some are still persecuted by those Outside. Some come as children; all come in childlike faith. They come for the hope, the relief, the eternal blessings inside the tent. They—we—have charted a common course. And whatever the destination, whatever the precise details, we will be "in Christ," from now, till then, till the age beyond.

It'll all add up just fine.

*D*o you know why God uses mystery?

Because He is a God at play.

Don't get me wrong. I don't mean to demean God or try to bring Him down to our level or to that of a child. I think of play as a good thing, something strong and mature. And mystery is playful and creative. It lures another person forward, coaxing interest and kneading curiosity. Mystery builds tension, then enjoys the release of discovery. It rewards faith with discovery and insight.

That's why God enjoys mystery. A bit coyly, God leads us eagerly into the future, keeping us expectant. What will it look like to see everything summed up in Christ? What will heaven and earth convey when brought together? Can't you just feel God's eagerness to show us?

History is pockmarked with tragedies, but God has laced the ages with joy as well. He has filled the Sanctuary with an underlying sense of anticipation, expectation, and longing. And why should we be surprised? The Creator is creative! And playful. Even Jesus said He didn't know the time of the Second Coming (Matthew 24:36). The Father is keeping even Jesus fascinated with the adventure.

Thank You, God, for mystery. Then. Now. Later.

And probably forever. I know the Bible promises, "Now we see but a poor reflection as in a mirror; then we shall see face to face" (1 Corinthians 13:12). But I rather expect that seeing face to face will be *relative* clarity—more insight than we have now—but God (if I understand Him at all) will still have that glimmer in His eye, that playful love for the intriguing. Do we really expect to *ever* be on par with God, knowing absolutely everything He knows? In heaven, we'll have glorified bodies and minds, but we'll still be His creations, still blessed to look to Him in admiration and praise. Maybe the reason we'll be with Him forever is because it will take Him that long to play out the mystery!

When I married Lyn, a friend approached me at the reception and said, "Bob, you've married over your head!" He implied that I married a bride much more beautiful than I merited. (His implication was correct.) Now, as I've delved into Sanctuary life, I've been *writing* over my head. (Please don't say, "I can tell!" You can think it; just don't say it.) I guess that's how mystery works. We try to describe images we can't clearly see through the window, forms that hide partially in the mist. The best window squeegee we have is prayer, but even when we pray, the window seems to keep fogging up.

Some say we should only write or preach about truths we have experienced, but I don't agree. (If I did, my repertoire of sermons would be pretty limited.) Instead, we must try to describe the indescribable, to fathom the unfathomable.

The peak of the mountain, and even an occasional glimpse of it, keeps us climbing.

Jesus Christ revealed the mystery, but He still mystifies. He has explained God, yet He defies explanation. He's our God who could snuff out humanity with a snap of two fingers, yet our Friend who would sit beside us in the dirt and weep about our disappointments. The Sanctuary is our present reality, but it's also nebulous, and we wonder sometimes if we've missed something. The way I see it, there's still a lot of mystery left.

Back to my admission: Some truths are so high I can only point the way and say, "They're somewhere up there." I wish I could lead you by the hand like an experienced guide who knows the trail by heart. But I'm only a fellow traveler. Not far into the climb, I have to say. "Take His hand, as I have, and let's see where He leads us."

This is bittersweet. While I find it frustrating to see so dimly, I can't imagine it any other way here on earth. If God is God, there ought to remain some mystery. If you and I could walk up to God and look Him eye-to-eye as equals, we would have lost our most precious right: our right to worship. We would possess no higher focus than ourselves. And that would be terrible.

So let's carry on. Let's recognize that Sanctuary living will always elude us, will always require faith. Let's accept the fact that the loose ends aren't neatly tied together, that many of our questions still need answers.

Let's remember that while the sum isn't yet totaled, while the groaning of creation is not yet an "Aahh" of relief and rapture, it will be someday. Someday soon.

*God of the ages,*

*sometimes my future seems like a toddler wandering out onto a busy street.*

*Aimless. At risk. Ignorant of the hazards.*

*I confess my fears.*

*I fear that I'll naively walk into a trap*

*or that someone I love will be taken from me.*

*I fear squealing brakes followed by the crash of my plans or my work.*

*Thank You that in Christ I'm not that aimless child.*

*Thank You that You hold my hand, Father,*

*that You see the hazards and will guide me as You deem best.*

*And that You hold the mystery I can't now understand,*

*the mystery You will reveal in Your time,*

*the grand mystery of living in Your Sanctuary.*

# Selah
# Golgotha

**Selah (Hebrew):** *means "meditations," as in Psalm 19:14.*
*Its usual position is either at the end of a strophe or of a psalm.*
**Golgotha (Aramaic):** *"skull," also translated "place of a skull;"*
*name of an eminence near Jerusalem, used as a place of execution.*

Helen Colijn detested the jungle's hot mugginess. Her confinement to a refugee camp in Sumatra with hundreds of other women and girls made it worse. With no more space than a football field, and no freedom beyond the barbed-wire fence, Helen felt trapped.

And alone. Her father had been taken to a different camp. She didn't know her mother's whereabouts. Only her two young sisters were with her.

Helen was twenty-two. The place was the Dutch East Indies during World War II. The conditions were deplorable. The inadequate food supply took its toll in the form of emaciated bodies and rampant sickness. Clothes wore thin, along with patience. Dysentery and malaria reduced the ranks of those rounded up and hounded down by brutal guards.

But one day, Helen began to notice a mood change in the camp. Some of the girls began to smile. Some of the women reflected hope in their eyes. They couldn't possibly foresee imminent release, so why this emergence of optimism?

Helen couldn't have anticipated the explanation. How could she? Who would have imagined a concert in the middle of squalor?

It was a sight to behold. In shoes worn and dirty, the choir shuffled into the open air "pavilion." They carried scraps of paper that consititued their musical score. Thirty women filed into the fenced space behind their leader, Norah Chambers, who had studied at the Royal Academy of Music in London. They called themselves an "orchestra," and what they performed that day was a collection of the world's great instrumental arrangements…without the instruments! You see, Norah and a Presbyterian missionary named Margaret Dryburgh had penned these pieces from memory and arranged them for a four-part orchestra of voices.

The concert began with the dignified strength of Antonin Dvořák's *New World Symphony.* And the music brought a refreshment for which the women had starved. It took little imagination to actually hear violins. Required no effort to envision the gleaming trumpets. As the women played Chopin's "Raindrop Prelude," Helen recalled a concert in the Netherlands where she had met the boy who took her on her first date. Debussy's "Reverie" carried her back to a formal evening in long dress with her father by her side.

At one point in the concert, a gruff guard entered the camp through the back fence. Furious, he worked his way to the front. Norah heard the commotion but continued directing. As the guard proceeded forward, the crowd closed behind him, and Helen couldn't see his actions. She only knew what *didn't* happen. The guard didn't stop the music. Somehow along the way, his grumpiness must have melted. The concert not only continued, but the guard sat through it, perhaps himself reminded of better times.

What had transpired in that remote internment camp was a miracle of the human spirit. The music replaced what the filthy rats and smelly latrines had begun to steal. Years later, after the camp was dismantled and the women released, one woman wrote to Helen, "When I sang, I forgot I was in the camp. I felt free."[1]

Why do we sometimes find the most intense beauty in the midst of ugliness? A dandelion is never so alluring as when it grows from a mound of discarded rubbish. A colorful mural is uncommonly pretty when painted on a wall within a concrete jungle.

Men in dinner jackets and women in floor-length gowns have enjoyed

Chopin and Handel hundreds of times, but a concert of voices in Sumatra one afternoon far surpassed the most superb symphony ever heard in any European music hall.

God has placed in our hearts a longing for beauty, and when beauty must fight for expression against great odds, it's all the more precious. Perhaps the sheer effort moves us. When I see a fast runner at the peak of fitness cross a finish line first, I react with admiration. But when I watch the last person cross the finish line, perhaps a bit overweight or hampered by some bodily weakness, yet straining and determined all the same, I cry. You and I well up with tears and swallow hard because, while the winner was good, the last guy was beautiful. And then we wonder who *really* won the race.

From history's most despicable ugliness, our world's most wondrous beauty has emerged. From time's most heinous crime of deception and theft has come forth eternity's loveliest love. Only one Man in all time could climb Golgotha and create a work of art. And He did. Only one God in all eternity could build a Sanctuary where Devastation reigned. He did that too.

As Helen Colijn discovered, depravation spawns creativity. Poverty calls forth ingenuity. Some of the greatest creativity in the world belongs to people who own nothing. I've seen playground cars made of wire, traveling on bottle-cap wheels, created by shoeless boys dressed in rags. Those boys are miles ahead of the clean-smelling lad who pulled his toy car out of a box.

I've seen houses built from flattened tin cans, held together by reclaimed nails and secondhand boards scavenged from the junk piles of the rich. I never knew how useful a tin can could be. And how about the folks around the world who sell gum or biscuits or cigarettes out of a "store" constructed of cardboard? Well, all I can say is they're ingenious. Those buildings are as creative as Dvořák in a refugee camp. And nearly as beautiful as a wooden bridge shaped like a cross, spanning the gulf between despair and delight.

I wonder. Are you surrounded by a string of barbed wire, thirsting for refreshment? Would your eyes fall closed in delight to hear a strain of deep music of the soul? Let Jesus be the concert hall in your parched place. May His truth wash over your hurting spirit like a cleansing shower. May your barrenness and loneliness qualify you for a most unexpected wonder.

# Third
# Hymn

# The Uncluttered View from Olivet
## Our Safety in the Son

And you also were included in Christ

when you heard the word of truth,

the gospel of your salvation.

Having also believed, you were marked in him with a seal,

the promised Holy Spirit,

who is a deposit guaranteeing our inheritance

until the redemption of those who are God's possession—

to the praise of his glory.

EPHESIANS 1:13–14

How little we knew that when Jesus promised the Spirit

He guaranteed us permanent life in Himself.

*J*esus was leading His eleven disciples through the Kidron Valley just east of Jerusalem. On their way toward the Mount of Olives, He paused to pray in a grove of trees known as Gethsemane.

As they walked, the apostle John wrote feverishly. This guy was amazing. Not to diminish the role of divine inspiration (and likely, recall), but anybody who can write eighty-six verses of Scripture while walking at night through vineyards and orchards deserves some kind of award for tenacity (John 15–17). John could have been a war correspondent! He must have stayed over Jesus' shoulder the whole hike, must have had a photographic memory, and (sorry if I'm wrong on this one, John) must have peeked during the prayer! That's right, John 17 was either scribbled messily by a closed-eyed apostle or written legibly by a peek-sneaking one!

More to the point, Jesus had announced over dinner that He was going somewhere the disciples couldn't follow, and they found this thought sobering. The Lord knew their feelings, and He wanted to encourage them. Perhaps as He led His friends through a vineyard overlooking the river, the perfect analogy came to Him. But whether it happened that way isn't the important point. What matters is what He said to them, "I am the true vine, and my Father is the gardener" (John 15:1).

I doubt if this solitary statement pulled the disciples out of their doldrums. I doubt if the angels sang an eight-part arrangement of "Alleluia!" But as Jesus unveiled His word picture, I'll bet the disciples' ears started to perk up. "Remain in me, and I will remain in you" (John 15:4). Stay connected to the Vine, and the Vine won't let go of you.

Two things result from this connection. As Christ had already said, remain in Jesus, and (result one) He will remain in you. Now for result two: "If a man remains in me and I in him, he will bear much fruit" (John 15:5).

If Jesus had made this statement with a vineyard close by, it would have rendered his point undebatable. The leaves were probably green, and the boughs may have been laden with bunches of purple grapes.

As a side point, Jesus might have directed their attention to a pile of brown trimmings nearby. The dry and lifeless leaves would testify to Jesus' truth: "No branch can bear fruit by itself. Neither can you bear fruit unless you remain in me" (John 15:4). Again, two results: If you don't remain in Jesus, (result one) you won't bear fruit, and (result two) you'll be pruned.

So the disciples needed no more convincing. Abiding in Jesus was definitely the way to go. "No arguments, Lord. Just this one little problem. You seem to be planning a fairly long journey. How do we stay connected with You when You're nowhere to be found?" (John, don't slow down. Be sure to get the answer to this one.)

I don't know if Jesus stated this all at once or if He paused now by a log and then by a tree to make His various points. Furthermore, I don't think His response cleared up all their confusion. But I do know this: Jesus started talking a lot about the Holy Spirit. From this point on, the Holy Spirit was one of Christ's major themes. Let me give you some excerpts from John's quill pen:

> When the Counselor comes, whom I will send to you from the Father, the Spirit of truth who goes out from the Father, he will testify about me. (John 15:26)
>
> It is for your good that I am going away. Unless I go away, the Counselor will not come to you; but if I go, I will send him to you. (John 16:7)
>
> I have much more to say to you, more than you can now bear. But when he, the Spirit of truth, comes, he will guide you into all truth. (John 16:12–13)

The disciples likely kept scratching their heads about this until the Day of Pentecost, but at least Jesus had clarified that He would provide a way to stay connected with Him even though the current arrangement would change.

Now advance your time clock by about forty days. Jesus and His disciples had returned to the same olive groves. The pile of pruned vines had been burned. The disciples could look out the corners of their eyes and see Gethsemane, where they learned the embarrassing lesson about vigilance in prayer. (If you recall, they couldn't seem to stay awake.) Jesus had risen from death and was about to leave them as promised. May I employ the tool of understatement by saying it wasn't one of those really happy moments?

Yet the event that transpired on the Mount of Olives left the disciples encouraged! An hour or so later they were recharged. They descended the hill worshiping and joyful and fully committed to prayer (Luke 24:52; Acts 1:14).

What had happened? Jesus gave them perspective, *His* perspective. He reminded the disciples that the Holy Spirit would show up soon. He reiterated that they would receive the get-up-and-go to get up and go! And He said He would return after (by African time) just a little while (Acts 1:6–11).

You see, Olivet isn't a noble mountain, but it offers a spectacular view. And the key to enjoying the sight is to believe just as far as His eyes can see.

# CHAPTER SEVEN

# Safe and Sound

*Do you feel threatened by anything today?*

Everything was "business as usual" that day. The sun shone over Nairobi. And, as dictated by her daily routine, Barb Butler drove to the bus stop to pick up her kids after school.

But then the day took a most unusual and frightening turn. As the first parent to arrive at the bus stop, perhaps Barb was an easy target. A man approached her car from behind, walked past it, then turned back. Barb could see trouble coming. The man approached her window, pulled a revolver from his business suit, and pointed it at her head through the window. Opening the door, he told her to move over, but she was shaking uncontrollably and could hardly move her legs. He shoved her over and opened the back doors for two accomplices to get into the backseat.

The gun-toting driver handed his weapon to one of his friends and drove off. "Where are your kids?" he demanded. She said she had been waiting for them when the men hijacked her car. "Do you want to get them?" Unable to think straight, she said, "Yes, I would." The driver pretended to turn around to pick up the kids, but then he drove in another direction.

Then the driver said, "It's time to start praying because you're going to die." The man in the backseat held the gun on Barb. She started praying—aloud: "Dear Lord, I thank You that You love me…" And as she prayed those words, the strangest thing happened. Barb felt a warm light descend on her, as if God had literally sent His love from heaven in a cozy and comforting hug. In a most unusual way, Barb was sealed from the danger around her, at peace in this most disturbing situation. She felt that God was taking her home.

When Barb told me this story, I couldn't help but think of God's goodness amid a frightening situation. What better picture could there be of a peace "which transcends all understanding" (Philippians 4:7)?

After this peaceful embrace, Barb became freshly aware of her surroundings. One of the men demanded all her money. She had only sixteen shillings— less than a dollar. Though the men were stealing a car worth thousands of dollars, they pilfered her small change! Then they demanded that she give them her wedding ring. On instinct, she refused. "You'll have to get it off yourself," she said, clenching her left fist. They abandoned the idea of taking the ring.

Then the driver glanced at the gun-wielding accomplice. "Not in the head," he instructed. Barb tried to advance the argument: "If you shoot me, you'll get blood all over the car." The driver repeated, "Not in the head." Barb grimaced, expecting a shot in the back.

But it never came. Instead, the driver pulled over and, almost as quickly as she had been hijacked, Barb was released. She ran from the car, free.

Safety. Can we really hope for any such thing in this crazy world? This morning I watched a bird gathering bits of grass for a new nest. After collecting each piece, the bird looked around for any possible danger. Is that how we must live life, never able to relax and feel safe?

A couple of my buddies have shared with me feelings they're still processing about their growing-up years. Their two tales share a similar theme: Neither of them grew up in the safe environment they so desperately needed. Now, neither of these friends were raised on the streets. They didn't have alcoholic parents. In fact, both grew up in Christian homes. So why the lack of safety? Well, one of my friends had an angry father who often spanked him harshly for failing to obey strict standards. My other friend lacked emotional stability at home. He never knew where he stood with his parents. Never experienced intimacy. Enjoyed no freedom to share feelings and receive comfort and affirmation. He desperately needed a safe retreat from the threatening world, but home only brought him more insecurity.

Let's not bluff each other in this chapter. We live in a real world with real risks. Tragedies happen, and they don't spare Christians. We can't say that if we trust God nothing bad will happen to us. Talk to the pastor who lost his wife and kids in a car wreck. Talk to the deaconess who was robbed. Interview the sweet, eighty-year-old lady in my first congregation who was beaten and raped in her home. Then let's tuck those pious platitudes right back in our holey pockets where they belong. We live in a dangerous world, and we're *all* vulnerable.

So when I talk about safety, I don't mean that we can somehow live in some indestructible haven that danger cannot infiltrate. Rather, I refer to an inner peace that no threatening situation can steal away. I have in mind a deep safety, a security of the heart, a guarantee that what really counts cannot be lost.

Take Barb Butler's experience. The gunman could have pulled the trigger. The day that began so normally could have been her last. But even amid this dreadful possibility, God gave Barb a special representation of His presence, a comforting reminder of His nearness in that frightful hour. In the midst of chaos, God assured Barb that she was truly safe, threatened in circumstance but secure in Him. The thieves were in apparent control, but God was there to guard what really mattered.

## The Master's Mark

Which brings us back to the Sanctuary. Everything we really need is there. All we can truly keep is there too. Real safety—not the situational kind but the spiritual and eternal variety—rises or falls with the security of our life in Jesus Christ. We can now appreciate the significance of the third hymn's lyrics:

> And you also were included in Christ when you heard the word of truth, the gospel of your salvation. Having believed, you were marked in him with a seal, the promised Holy Spirit, who is a deposit guaranteeing our inheritance until the redemption of those who are God's possession—to the praise of his glory. (Ephesians 1:13–14)

You see, God thought of everything. Not only has He...

blessed us with every spiritual blessing in His Son (Ephesians 1:3);
chosen us in His Son (Ephesians 1:4, 11);

predestined us to be adopted through His Son (Ephesians 1:5, 11);

redeemed us in His Son (Ephesians 1:7); and

established plans to sum up all things in His Son (Ephesians 1:10);

but God the Father has insured our safety by keeping us in His Son by the protective seal of the Holy Spirit. The third and final hymn of the Sanctuary, like its predecessors, advances the theme of our life in Christ. We were "included in Christ" and "marked in him with a seal" (Ephesians 1:13). Worship in Christ's body celebrates yet another priceless treasure supplied us in Jesus.[1]

Dwellers in the caves of insecurity such as you and I need to hear again and again the melodious message of this hymn.

For starters, *the protective seal was a need the Father foresaw and, therefore, something He promised.* We've grown so accustomed to surviving on our own, to fighting viciously for and clinging protectively to our acquisitions, that we find it hard to imagine someone else taking on that responsibility for us. Let's face it, every little child learns that the most useful word on the playroom floor is *mine!* By nature, toddlers see what they want and, oftentimes with a whack and most times with a grab, yell, "Gimmedat!" As we grow into adulthood, our methods become more sophisticated but no less selfish; we find a way to acquire and keep what we think we need and what we know we want.

With this as our usual modus operandi, isn't it a shock to discover that when it comes to Sanctuary riches, God is a step ahead of us? That He wants to take care of us and give us exactly what we need?

That's exactly what He has done, and that's why He promised us the Holy Spirit.

Just before Jesus ascended to heaven, He had a little dinner conversation with the disciples about what they should expect in the time to come. He gave them this command: "Do not leave Jerusalem, but wait for the gift my Father promised, which you have heard me speak about. For John baptized with water, but in a few days you will be baptized with the Holy Spirit" (Acts 1:4–5).

The disciples had a tough job ahead of them: Sharing the Good News with the world. They needed guidance and encouragement, and they knew it. They also had a few other needs, ones they didn't know about. But the Father knew about them. He knew, to be specific, that the life of discipleship would consist of life in Christ, so He promised the disciples a Spirit who would place believers as adopted children into Christ and would keep them there forever.

And so the Father created two baptisms, each a distinct expression of His loving provision. John the Baptist's baptism would acknowledge pure hearts for salvation; the Father's promised baptism would empower hearts for service. Water baptism affirms entrance into the Sanctuary, while Spirit baptism enfolds us within it. The River Jordan confirmed the washing away of sin; the day of Pentecost gave hope for safety. And when delivered, the Holy Fulfillment was as big as the promise.

Perhaps you're wondering who receives this promise. Listen to the Sanctuary hymn. The second truth about the Holy Spirit addresses this very question: *The protective seal is the assurance of everyone who has heard and believed the gospel.*

You probably hoped for or expected something more complicated than that, but I'm just tuning our ears to the song, not embellishing it. Those sealed in Christ by the Holy Spirit share two simple experiences. One, they have heard the word of truth, the gospel of salvation. Two, they have believed it. It's so simple a child can do it. And many do!

Have you ever heard that Jesus Christ died for your sins, was buried, and on the third day rose to live forever? (You just read it, so say yes. You have now taken the first step toward being sealed in Christ!)

Have you believed that the above claims about Jesus are true, not just historically true but the truth you cling to for your own salvation? If so, great! Take a look in your mirror, and you'll see someone sealed forever in Christ Jesus by the Holy Spirit. That's right. You're the one! (If you haven't believed these truths, what stops you from taking that leap of faith now and enjoying eternal assurance of your place in Christ? You might want to discuss any questions and concerns with a local pastor or a Christian friend.)

## God's Word-Picture of Safety

Now that we understand that the Holy Spirit affirms the believer's place in Christ, we're ready to hear the third insight about the seal: *The protective seal is God's word-picture of our safety and security in His Son.*

From ancient times, people have needed indications of authority and authenticity. Think about it. When you buy a house or draw up your will, you take your papers to a notary public. The seal placed on your legal documents communicates that they are the real thing. And because they're the authentic documents, people must live by the claims made therein.

The need for such a seal of authority and authenticity didn't begin with our distrustful, present-day society. People in biblical times often used seals; for example, when the officials joined Nehemiah in pledging obedience to God, they all put their seals on the document stating their intentions (Nehemiah 10:1). They created their seals by pressing a signet ring—or rolling a cylinder that bore a special mark—into a blob of damp clay or wax that they then allowed to dry.

Seals in those days not only signified authenticity, they also secured and protected that which was sealed. Often, people would roll or fold a document, such as a will, then seal it so no one could read it.[2] Or they would mark a vessel or compartment with a seal, conveying the message, "Don't open or tamper with this container under penalty of the one whose seal marks it!" The lion's den (Daniel 6:18) and Jesus' tomb (Matthew 27:66) were closed with such protective seals. In these cases, only the owner of the seal could break it. (This is why, in Revelation 5:1–5, John wept until Jesus showed up; only He could open the sealed scroll.)

With this background, let's return to the hymn and allow the refrain to sink in a little deeper: "Having believed, you were marked in him with a seal, the promised Holy Spirit" (Ephesians 1:13). All who have believed in Jesus have been placed in the Sanctuary. God has guaranteed our protection by placing on us His seal, the Holy Spirit. We can't seal ourselves or manipulate someone or something into sealing us. *God seals us.*[3] And He only needs to do it once: When we believe what we have heard.[4]

How can we summarize the significance of God's seal? Let's put it this way. Our Father loves each of His children so much that He puts us in the safest place in the universe: His Son. This is such a safe place because His Son overcame everything that could have threatened us: the lion of devastation, death, and hell. Then to ensure that each of us will safely remain in that safest of places, our loving God seals us inside His Son using the strongest substance ever known: the powerful Holy Spirit.

And so, day by day, the holy Trinity joyfully creates an eternal "love package" for their own delight. They bring us, one by one, into the Sanctuary, wrap us in forgiveness and full acceptance in Christ, and hold us within their sovereign, eternal love. Using a different metaphor but making the same point, Jesus once said, "I give them eternal life, and they shall never perish; no one can snatch them out of my hand. My Father, who has given them to me, is greater than all; no one can snatch them out of my Father's hand" (John 10:28–29).

As those who have heard the truthful word and have believed it, we are the safest, most secure beings ever to live. We are precisely as safe as Jesus is. Our life is in Him, and wherever He goes, we go. Whatever power He possesses works to protect us. The Holy Spirit prevents against any attrition, for as a vigilant guard, He seals us in Christ.

No wonder the Bible says that nothing can separate us from God's love! That would require extracting either love or us from Jesus' heart. Since neither we nor love will leave the Sanctuary, we can believe that God's love is our permanent companion (Romans 8:35–39).

Do you feel threatened by anything today? If so, what intruders seem to loom outside the windows of your life? Let's not belittle their significance. The world is a dangerous place. Robbers can steal our belongings. Other criminals can kidnap a priceless child or snuff out a precious life. Any sane person understands and dreads these threats. We pray and protect ourselves against them.

But view these real dangers against the backdrop of life in Christ. What is a stolen necklace when compared with all spiritual riches? What is a burned house when contrasted with an eternal home in Christ? And even if the worst should happen, that which you most strongly dread—such as losing the people you love most or even your own life to an accident, dreaded disease, or insane gunman— would that dreadful experience remove you from the Sanctuary? Could the worst of human experiences drive any of us from the garden of God's love? No way. Read Christ's promise again: "I give them eternal life, and they shall never perish; no one can snatch them out of my hand. My Father, who has given them to me, is greater than all; no one can snatch them out of my Father's hand" (John 10:28–29).

You see, fear is relative. We tend to fear things that happen in the visible world, but the really scary experiences happen in the now-invisible, heavenly realm. Jesus told us not to fear those who can harm the body but instead to revere God, who can cast both soul and body in hell (Matthew 10:28). We can attempt to protect ourselves by posting armed guards around our houses and by eating well and exercising so we have the healthiest bodies in the world, but if we aren't "in Christ," we're in imminent danger.

Conversely, when we reside within the Sanctuary because we believe in Christ's death on the cross, we can walk through dangerous neighborhoods, go into battle, and suffer debilitating diseases—yet remain the safest of earth's inhabitants. Nothing and no one can harm Sanctuary dwellers.

*R*ight now, consider that which you fear losing. Is it a person or a group of loved ones? If so, write down his, her, or their names. Is it your health? Then jot that down too. Is it a livelihood, a ministry, a dream, or a goal? Whatever you fear losing, include it on your list.

Now take a good look at your list. As you do, bring each item, one by one, into the Sanctuary, and look at it afresh. How does your dream measure up to all your heavenly blessings in Christ? How vital is good health when placed alongside your permanent adoption by your Abba? The loved ones you couldn't stand to lose—are they in Christ, by faith, like you? If so, then you can't really lose them; you might endure a temporary separation, but you won't lose them forever. (This is excellent incentive to share the Sanctuary with those who don't know about it yet.) Earth's pain is real, but it will pass with a few sweeps of a watch's second hand. Eternal joy is real too, and a watch's hour hand cannot measure the most infinitesimal fraction of it.

The Sanctuary puts fear in perspective. Barb Butler caught a glimpse of that perspective. In the face of imminent physical harm, her safety in the Sanctuary enveloped her, embracing her with a peace that could come only from the seal of Jesus Christ. She had everything to lose, and absolutely nothing to lose.

See what I mean about mystery?

*Incredible! Amazing!*

*These words flood my mind, Lord, as I realize how safe*

*You want me to feel.*

*I've lived too long under a deceptive illusion,*

*thinking I was only an accident or heartbeat away from losing everything.*

*Thank You that I don't have to be deluded anymore.*

*Help me to live within this newly discovered reality of*

*my ultimate safety in You.*

# CHAPTER EIGHT

# Your Rustproof Inheritance

*We are princes living like criminals.*
*Monarch butterflies crawling like ugly worms.*
*We need a stiff reminder of who we are: heirs!*

Every woman of ancient Israel wanted just one thing. If she could have nothing else, this one item would fulfill her. Like a credit card on a journey or a health insurance plan during illness, Hebrew women in biblical times didn't want to lack this bare necessity: a husband.

When a woman of those times married, she gained a name and an identity. Through her husband, she also procured land, and land in those days was vital. Land gave a person a home, a livelihood, and therefore, a future. And landowners commanded respect and position within the community.

But some landowners lost their property and with it the benefits of ownership. Some didn't farm their land well and had to sell it just to survive. Others ran up debt and had to forfeit some or all of their land to pay their creditors. In a woman's case, if her husband died and she had no sons, she had no one to tend her land and therefore no source of income, a circumstance that threatened her land and her livelihood.

Losing land caused another far-reaching consequence: loss of inheritance. In agrarian societies such as ancient Israel, a father passed on his identity and his "place" by giving each of his sons a portion of his land. In receiving this, his sons received more than a piece of real estate. Rather, the inherited farm constituted the opportunity and responsibility to carry on the family name, to take the father's niche in the society, and to raise children who would continue the family's heritage. You see, the inheritance was everything. It was a father's hope for leaving a legacy beyond his years. It was a son's chance to make his own mark. And it was a mother's basis for security.

With that as background, I'd like to take you to an ancient place directed by these cultural mores. In this place, we find a wife who has lost her security. Her security's name had been Mahlon.

Her name was Ruth, a name Jews would find foreign, and for good reason: Ruth *was* a foreigner. Ruth came from Moab, a country that had constantly maintained hostile relations with Israel since the days of the judges. Ruth's foreignness complicates the story even further, but I'm getting ahead of myself.

## An Old-Fashioned Love Story

Ruth looked skyward from the grainfield in the middle of the day, wiped her brow against the effects of the hot sun, and lamented the chain of events that had led her to such humiliation. If her sister-in-law Orpah still had a husband, things would be different. If Naomi's husband was still alive, all three women would enjoy a livelihood from their land. But all three of them had been widowed by the harsh times of famine. And none of them had a son.

Because she loved her mother-in-law, Naomi, Ruth had moved from her beloved Moab to her deceased husband's homeland at this grievous, hopeless time. And here she was in someone else's field, gathering up scraps of barley left by the harvesters. Herself a landowner by inheritance, Ruth could not farm her own land, and she'd likely lose it. She would most definitely starve before she could grow her own food. So, as she mopped her forehead, she probably bid adieu to her land and farewell to her inheritance and the hope it promised.

In many modern societies, an inheritance is a short-lived financial boost people enjoy as they reach midlife, a familial "bonus" that helps pay for college or for a larger home. Many don't even expect to receive even this much of an inheritance. So an inheritance may not carry the force for you and me that it did for Ruth.

But while cultures and customs change, human need doesn't. While you and I may not need land, we appreciate security, a livelihood, and an honorable name. Like Ruth and her peers, we strive to be somebody, to make others proud, to belong and have a say.

As part of life in the Sanctuary, the Bible promises us a personal inheritance from God. We can spend an earthly inheritance in a matter of months, but an eternal inheritance is truly the gift that keeps on giving!

That's easy to say. But do you ever worry that you've jeopardized your inheritance from God? Ever hope you haven't disqualified yourself as an heir? Ever simply lack the faith to envision your spiritual inheritance as a real thing?

If you struggle with those feelings, you can probably relate to Ruth's predicament. Like you, Ruth wrestled with the reality of her inheritance. It was beginning to look illusory. And her ambition wasn't as grand as an *eternal* inheritance. She just wanted to keep her husband's farm. (She also didn't mind eating!)

Her mother-in-law held identical desires. And as a Jew, Naomi knew that God's law made one provision for a widow to retain her inheritance. There was one way, though a bit tricky and not just a little risky, for a woman to stay secure.

How? To find a kinsman-redeemer.

I'll explain this as long as you don't go out and try it yourself. According to God's law, Ruth could retain her inheritance if one of her husband Mahlon's near relatives would marry her (keep in mind that this relative, a Jew, had to be willing to take a Moabitess as a wife). This relative would then have to meet Ruth's needs and try to provide her a son who would bear Mahlon's name and cultivate the Mahlon family farm. Hence the term *kinsman-redeemer:* this person had to be a kinsman willing to redeem Ruth from her disinherited and bleak condition.

Because of her circumstances, Ruth would likely have been satisfied with a kinsman who would fulfill this role from cultural obligation. She probably didn't even hope that this man would love her. Regardless, securing a kinsman-redeemer was tricky business. Think about it. What was Ruth supposed to do, hold a big party for the clan and make an announcement? Send out invitations? Write up a résumé? Then, as now, someone who said "I'm available" was immediately considered undesirable. No, Ruth's situation called for coy wisdom and an intimate knowledge of acceptable ways to maneuver in sticky courtship situations.

Enter Naomi. "Now Naomi had a relative on her husband's side, from the clan of Elimelech, a man of standing, whose name was Boaz" (Ruth 2:1). You should read the entire Book of Ruth yourself sometime, because I can't do it justice. We don't know who wrote it, but I'm guessing the author is female simply because it's a great love story, something men generally have a tougher time writing. In context, even the verse above makes your heart flutter just a bit. Ruth needed a relative on her husband's side. She needed him to be the honorable and compassionate sort. And Naomi knew of a relative, "a man of standing," and his name even means "In him is strength." By now, the writer has every reader hoping that Boaz will be the guy for Ruth!

The story gets even better. Boaz turns out to be the most sterling chap you'd ever hope for. He saw Ruth gleaning in his field (that word means Ruth combed the fields for food the harvesters left for the poor people). Boaz told Ruth to help herself and to return as often as she wanted. He said she shouldn't glean in any other fields, only his, and he even offered her some food and ensured that no one hassled her. Was love blooming? Stay tuned.

Hearing of Boaz's kindness to Ruth, Naomi encouraged Ruth to enact a Jewish custom that enabled a widow to suggest her availability for marriage. When Naomi explained it to Ruth, according to the account, Ruth responded, "I will do whatever you say" (Ruth 3:5).

Following her mother-in-law's instructions, Ruth went by night to the threshing floor, the place where farmers ground the barley from the chaff. The landowner, in this case Boaz, always slept there during threshing time so no one could steal his grain. So after dinner, Ruth found the place where Boaz slept (sounds of snoring here). Then, according to Naomi's instructions, she "uncovered his feet and lay down" (Ruth 3:7).

I repeat: Don't try this yourself! We don't do things this way today. However, such actions were perfectly acceptable in the time and culture of Ruth, Naomi, and Boaz. In effect, Ruth asked Boaz in a socially acceptable manner to act as her kinsman-redeemer and take her as his wife. And what happened next is so good I have to quote it for you:

> In the middle of the night something startled the man [I can imagine!],
> and he turned and discovered a woman lying at his feet.
>     "Who are you?" he asked.

"I am your servant Ruth," she said. "Spread the corner of your garment over me, since you are a kinsman-redeemer."

"The Lord bless you, my daughter," he replied. "This kindness is greater than that which you showed earlier: You have not run after the younger men, whether rich or poor. And now, my daughter, don't be afraid. I will do for you all you ask. All my fellow townsmen know that you are a woman of noble character." (Ruth 3:8–11)

Sounds like the fantasy of a few guys I know! But seriously, this is the story of a noble woman requesting an honorable man's help in protecting her family's inheritance. When Ruth covered herself with a bit of Boaz's garment, she communicated her desire to be covered by the security of his strength in the clan. And he willingly complied. What a story!

A happy ending seems imminent, doesn't it? But like the best love stories, this one has a twist: Boaz wasn't first in line to marry Ruth. That option belonged to the nearest kinsman. If that unnamed relative wanted to marry Ruth, Boaz would have to settle for the role of best man. But the story has a happy ending after all. The other guy wanted the land but didn't feel he could handle the lady (Ruth 4:1–6). So he declined and invited Boaz to act as redeemer. The relative did this in a fascinating and traditional way: He removed one of his sandals and handed it to Boaz. In so doing, he legalized the transaction, saying in effect, "I have no claim on the land or on Ruth. You have the right to walk on the land. It's yours."

When Boaz gripped that sandal, Ruth gained a husband and retained her inheritance. She had security. She had a future. And she even won Boaz's love!

It might seem an awfully long leap from a threshing floor in ancient Judah to a hymn in the Sanctuary of Jesus today, but it's actually an easy, automatic jump. Ruth's story tells the tale of a disinherited foreigner fortunate enough to find rescue from her plight through the kindness of one uniquely qualified to redeem her situation.

Sound familiar?

Ruth's story is your story…only yours is even better. You have a better land, a better inheritance, and even a better Husband.

## Blessed Assurance!

Fanny Crosby was a prolific hymn writer who lacked physical sight but possessed incredible spiritual perception. She had no trouble envisioning her heavenly Husband when she wrote:

> Blessed assurance, Jesus is mine!
> Oh, what a foretaste of glory divine!
> Heir of salvation, purchase of God,
> Born of His Spirit, washed in His blood.
> This is my story, this is my song,
> Praising my Saviour all the day long.[1]

Compared to Jesus, Boaz had it easy. Boaz had a few additional mouths to feed, but Jesus had a life to forfeit. "For this reason Christ is the mediator of a new covenant, *that those who are called may receive the promised eternal inheritance—now that he has died* as a ransom to set them free from the sins committed under the first covenant" (Hebrews 9:15, emphasis mine).

You and I have a Kinsman-Redeemer, Jesus Christ. He stepped in to redeem, not just because of duty but because He loves us. He stated his commitment not just by receiving a sandal but in accepting Golgotha's challenge. And now we have an inheritance! The Father has overseen and delighted in the whole transaction. Here's your very own Ruth-story in a New Testament nutshell:

> But when the kindness and love of God our Savior appeared, he saved us, not because of righteous things we had done, but because of his mercy. He saved us through the washing of rebirth and renewal by the Holy Spirit, whom he poured out on us generously through Jesus Christ our Savior, so that, having been justified by his grace, *we might become heirs having the hope of eternal life.* (Titus 3:4–7, emphasis mine)

We hear a recurring theme as we worship in the Sanctuary: Life in Jesus provides us everything we truly need. The Holy Spirit seals for us in Christ everything of real value. And now we add one more treasure to our chest because the Sanctuary is also where our inheritance lies. In fact, in the same way that Boaz was a part of Ruth's inheritance by loving her above and beyond buying rights to her field, so Jesus Himself is an integral part of our inheritance. Our inheritance isn't just what Jesus gains for us or what He gives us and keeps for us; it's what He *is* for us. He is the love of a husband. He is the flow of guidance and strength from a head to the body. He is the fullness for our every emptiness.

God hasn't revealed everything about our inheritance. He has told us enough to assure us and please us—and intrigue us. We know we stand to inherit everything that Jesus is. We know we'll never lack any single thing. But does that fully explain the inheritance? Not to me. What will the inheritance look like? Will I see it, or will I just feel it? You see, God is coy.

But let's focus on what we *do* know about our inheritance. For one thing, it's *permanent.* Peter wrote of it: "In his great mercy he has given us new birth into a living hope through the resurrection of Jesus Christ from the dead, and *into an inheritance that can never perish, spoil or fade*—kept in heaven for you" (1 Peter 1:3–4, emphasis mine).

For another thing, our inheritance is *generous.* Sometimes as people near the end of their lives and determine the inheritance they'll give to their loved ones, they think in terms of fairness: "How can I give my estate in proper proportions to reflect my appreciation (or lack thereof) for each one?" But when God chose heirs and planned their inheritance, He didn't think fairness; He thought generosity! "Listen, my dear brothers: Has not God chosen those who are poor in the eyes of the world to be *rich in faith* and to *inherit the kingdom* he promised those who love him?" (James 2:5, emphasis mine).

If you've ever given a present to a child who didn't expect one, you know why God delights to bless the disinherited. You know why He loves to give a secure future to those who despaired of tomorrow.

And as He planned His "will" He couldn't restrain Himself, so He gave every available blessing to every one of His children. This was a convenient way to handle it, for He just gave each of His children the embodiment of everything in His "estate": Christ. Jesus is our inheritance. He's the sum total of everything the Father has to give.

And in Christ, we stand to inherit substantially. In fact, don't ponder your inheritance in terms of individual items. Think vaults. There are at least four of them.

We might call one of the vaults "The Person of God." Perusing through it we will find:

- unity with God's spirit (1 Corinthians 6:17);
- a hiding place with Christ in God (Colossians 3:1–4; Hebrews 3:14);
- the Spirit of power, love, and discipline (2 Timothy 1:7); and
- a share in the divine nature (2 Peter 1:4).

We can label our second vault "A Place to Belong." It features:

- membership in Christ's body (1 Corinthians 12:27; Ephesians 5:30);
- citizenship in God's family and membership in His household (Ephesians 2:19); and
- a place as heirs according to the hope of eternal life (Titus 3:7).

Our third vault, "Relationship," contains:

- friendship with Christ (John 15:15);
- God's love (Colossians 3:12);
- access to God through the Spirit (Ephesians 2:18); and
- freedom to approach God in boldness and confidence (Ephesians 3:12).

"Gifts," our final vault, holds:

- complete absence of condemnation (Romans 8:1);
- protection from the devil (1 John 5:18);
- the mind of Christ (1 Corinthians 2:16);
- every spiritual blessing (Ephesians 1:3);
- redemption, forgiveness, and grace in abundance (Ephesians 1:6–8);
- cancellation of our certificate of debts (Colossians 2:14); and
- God's precious and magnificent promises (2 Peter 1:4).

Now grasp this: God predestined you to receive every one of these blessings. As soon as you heard and believed the word of truth, He activated your inheritance. The most trustworthy Judge read the papers in the courthouse of heaven, and upon your adoption all the assets of all the vaults were transferred immediately and fully to your account.

Nothing and no one can derail the process. The papers can't be misfiled. The document can't be questioned. For it's all "predestined according to the plan of him who works out everything in conformity with the purpose of his will" (Ephesians 1:11).

Like the edge of Boaz's garment, God has covered you with the vast protection, provision, and safety of the kingdom.

## God Stays Put

In the last chapter, we tuned in to the Sanctuary's third hymn and celebrated our inclusion in Christ when we hear and believe the gospel of our salvation. We learned that God has marked us in Christ with a seal, the promised Holy Spirit. We drew from those words the fact that, no matter what happens in our circumstances, we are safe in Christ.

As the hymn continues, its focus moves to the security of God's gift to us. We've seen the importance of an inheritance and considered some of the riches God has promised us. Now we need to examine the truth for which members of Christ's body praise Him. Let's pick up the climax of our final hymn....

> Having believed, you were marked in him with a seal, the promised Holy Spirit, who is a deposit guaranteeing our inheritance until the redemption of those who are God's possession—to the praise of his glory. (Ephesians 1:13–14)

Some people move a lot. College students seem to move from one apartment to another at a moment's notice, honing the task to a science. (The fact that their possessions consist of three outfits, a guitar, one pair of shoes, and a backpack may facilitate the endeavor.) Many MKs, whether military kids or missionary kids, will tell you they moved dozens of times during their childhood.

And certain jobs, whether in business or ministry, demand mobility. (I've lost count, but Lyn tells me we've moved twenty times in our twenty-two years of marriage. No wonder I'm dizzy!)

But God is different. He doesn't roam from place to place, staying just a few weeks or months before moving to a better arrangement. God moves in and stays put. And that's exactly what He has done with you. God's Spirit moved into you when you believed the Good News, and He has no intention of leaving. That action is God's pledge that He will deliver every single blessing He has promised you. It constitutes a "deposit guaranteeing our inheritance."

You'll probably laugh at me for this, but I just had a little "quiet time" while reading, of all things, a Greek dictionary! I looked up the word translated "deposit guaranteeing" (*arrabon*) and got pumped up by the security of my faith as I read the definition: "first installment, deposit, down payment, pledge, that pays a part of the purchase price in advance, and so *secures a legal claim to the article in question, or makes a contract valid…a payment which obligates the contracting party to make further payments*" (emphasis mine).[2]

Our spiritual inheritance is safe! All of it! The Holy Spirit is a first installment, a seal indicating authenticity and protection. And through the Spirit's presence, God promises that He will safely reserve for us all the vaults of His provision and that He will deliver them on time.

Nothing can steal away our inheritance. No cosmic police officers will ever come around after the fact, taking statements from witnesses, seeking to ascertain the whereabouts of our lost inheritance. Rust will not erode it and leave it as a pile of shavings on heaven's floor for angelic janitors, expressing condolences at our loss, to sweep up.

A passage in 2 Corinthians powerfully reinforces this truth. In fact, when I read these words I jotted down this summary: God never overpromises!

> For no matter how many promises God has made, they are "Yes" in Christ. And so through him the "Amen" is spoken by us to the glory of God. Now it is God who makes both us and you stand firm in Christ. He anointed us, set his seal of ownership on us, and put his Spirit in our hearts as a deposit, guaranteeing what is to come. (2 Corinthians 1:20–22)

If you think your diligence and effort secures your standing in Christ, don't flatter yourself. *God* is doing it! He has promised to make you stand firm in Christ, and He never overpromises.

Do you ever wish you had more than just the deposit? More than just the first installment? I do. Not that the deposit of the Holy Spirit is in any way inadequate, for none of us has ever fully drawn on the Spirit's power in our lives. But the realization that we have more coming makes us long for our *full* inheritance. God designed it that way so that we'd yearn for more, so that we'd long to be in His presence.

Scripture talks a lot about this yearning. It says our bodies "groan." Now I know that you might groan when you get out of bed in the morning. You groan after eating too much dinner. You groan when you know you have to perform an unpleasant task. But when the Bible talks about your body groaning, it refers to the uncomfortable strain of living with just a down payment. You see, a down payment both satisfies and frustrates. You're happy to have received it, but it also reminds you that you don't yet have the full payment. And if the down payment is sweet, the full payment will be scrumptious! As Paul wrote, the waiting can be as excruciating as childbirth pains, and "we ourselves, who have the firstfruits of the Spirit, groan inwardly as we wait eagerly for our adoption as sons, the redemption of our bodies" (Romans 8:23).

With the Spirit living inside us, we *taste* God's love and forgiveness. But our dull minds dilute the dose, and we long for the full payment, the full understanding of God's love for us. We long to feel the incredible sensation of being completely without condemnation.

Our Kinsman-Redeemer has opted to perform His duty. He has redeemed us and assured for us our inheritance. He has given us a down payment on our vaults of blessing. But in the future He'll step in and insist that we experience and realize the full implication of our redemption:

- He'll rescue our bodies from the sinful nature that now drags us through the dirt;
- He'll redeem our minds from the filth that stalks our holiest meditation;

- He'll deliver our hearts from the selfishness and pride that infiltrate our every motive;
- He'll heal us from every disease;
- Justice will reign rather than elude our collective grasp;
- Equality will come naturally rather than hide from us;
- Prejudice will vanish; and
- Hunger and poverty will cease to exist.

Don't be frustrated that we can't get our global act together. Don't be surprised that world bodies and powerful leaders can't remove earth's ills. Don't struggle against God's withholding full delivery of your inheritance for now. These things *can't* happen yet. We still face one major obstacle: "I declare to you, brothers, that flesh and blood cannot inherit the kingdom of God, nor does the perishable inherit the imperishable" (1 Corinthians 15:50).

Why just a down payment? Why not even half down, other half on delivery? Because the inheritance is so far beyond what we could now bear that God will have to radically change us so we can receive it. God has already anticipated this need: "Listen, I tell you a mystery: We will not all sleep, but we will all be changed" (1 Corinthians 15:51). Our incapacity to receive the inheritance in our present condition should remind us how great the full inheritance will be.

*W*hy do we live like paupers? What if Ruth, after her loving kinsman-redeemer restored her inheritance, had returned to the fields to glean grain just as those who—through bad luck or crushing debt—had become disinherited? And what if Ruth, still married to Boaz, found herself at night on another threshing floor in town with another landowner, appealing to him for marriage by slipping under the edge of his garment while he slept?

What would you think of Ruth if she did that? You'd wonder what kind of ingratitude or confusion had beset her. You'd wonder why she acted as if she had no inheritance. You'd wonder why, having received a love and a place and a name and a future, she continued to live like the pauper she once was.

Now take a gander at your church, your fellowship group, your family, yourself. Look at all of us. Our loving Kinsman-Redeemer has redeemed us. He has given us the largest inheritance ever granted in any courtroom, human or divine.

> For you did not receive a spirit that makes you a slave again to fear, but you received the Spirit of sonship. And by him we cry, "Abba, Father." The Spirit himself testifies with our spirit that we are God's children. *Now if we are children, then we are heirs—heirs of God and co-heirs with Christ,* if indeed we share in his sufferings in order that we may also share in his glory. (Romans 8:15–17, emphasis mine)

We have God's name written on our hearts. We have an eternal place, a right to belong in heaven. We have God's Son as our Friend, Co-heir, our very Inheritance. We have full forgiveness, complete acceptance, and the removal of all condemnation. And the Holy Spirit seals all this (and much more) for us in the Sanctuary of Jesus Christ.

With all this in hand, what do we do much of the time?

Glean for scraps.

We act like we've been disinherited, like we still need a redeemer:

- Instead of realizing we are dearly loved children of our Abba, we fail to even like ourselves;
- Instead of approaching our Father boldly in prayer, we trickle out apologetic remarks of our unworthiness;
- Instead of thankfully receiving His lavish grace, we drive ourselves to higher performance to prove our acceptability;
- Instead of believing that there is no condemnation for those in Christ Jesus, we condemn ourselves for our deficiencies;
- Instead of walking out of the prison doors of lust and inferiority that Christ has opened for us, we sit in the back of the cell looking forlorn and acting like captives;

- Instead of banking on God's promise of our grand, heavenly abode, we pour our lives into building earthly dwellings of wood and glass...or into envying those who do;
- Instead of feeding on God's rich Word, we blow the dust off our Bibles on our weekly trek to church;
- Instead of using the mind of Christ, we grovel around in the muck of self-pity or pornography;
- Instead of basking in the beauty of our salvation, we live with a doubtful hope of our worthiness;
- Instead of knowing that the devil cannot destroy us, we constantly look over our shoulders in fear of the lurking lion;
- And instead of believing that Christ has cancelled our debt, we wonder how in the world we can ever pay God for all the bad we've done.

We are rich oil barons acting as if we lost everything in a drunken poker game. Princes living like criminals. Monarch butterflies buzzing like gnats.

We need a stiff reminder of who we are: heirs! We have to remember that He said, "Yes, I'll redeem." Let's abandon the corners of the fields where we've collected leftovers and inhabit the full storehouse with its overflowing bins!

Pull out the title deed of your salvation and look at the Seal. Remember that God has already made the down payment and has safely stored the rest in the bank. Sing the song, *your* song, over and over. Insert your name in the hymn. (Go ahead, write it in, in permanent ink):

And I, _____, also was included in Christ when I heard the word of truth, the gospel of my salvation. Having believed, I, _____, was marked in Him with a seal, the promised Holy Spirit, who is a deposit guaranteeing my inheritance until my redemption as one who is God's possession—to the praise of his glory.

O Lord my God, when I consider how generous You've been toward me,

when I remember that I'm not the lowlife I often feel I am . . .

On the one hand,

I'm sorry for ignoring the incredible wealth You've given me.

I recognize the inconsistency of receiving the gift of the Holy Spirit

and living in fear and worry.

I want to live on the strong platform You've built for me

to abandon this puddle of discontent that soaks through my shoes.

On the other hand, I feel tremendous joy.

You've outdone yourself, God!

I long to be changed, to receive the fullness of my imperishable inheritance.

Thanks for holding it for me, Lord.

I'm holding on, too.

I'm holding on!

# Selah Olivet

**Selah (Hebrew):** *it may connect what precedes with what follows (sometimes by way of contrast) so as to stress both, as if to say, "This being so, give heed to what is now to be said." It often links one psalm with another, such as Psalms 3 and 4.*
**Olivet (Greek):** *"olive oil," used for lamps and for treating wounds; also translated "an olive orchard," specifically, the Mount of Olives or Olivet.*

There was a gang of men and women whose lives were dominated by Jesus Christ's promises. He had told them not to be overly concerned about *when* He would return but to get serious about their lives in the meantime. He had stood with them for the last time (until the next time) and promised them a powerful Spirit who would make them unstoppable living testimonies.

Then He had lifted up from that unimpressive mountain, and two fellows dressed in white told them not to worry because their Master had departed with a round-trip ticket.

And this little band of devotees was crazy enough to believe the whole story. So they went down the hill and changed the world.

Did they do it with their own talent and wisdom? Hardly. Remember, this same lot had vied for position and authority before the King of kings. They had fled and denied their Master when the showdown of Golgotha was heating up.

Did they change the world because their world was so small and receptive and eager for their message? No. Their Jerusalem was just as hostile as yours. Their Judea and Samaria were as pluralistic and deep-rooted in false beliefs as

yours. And their uttermost parts of the earth were every bit as distant and intimi-
dating as any you can think of today.

Then how do we explain what happened through this motley crew that lin-
gered in Olivet's shadow? Simply this. They discovered that the Overcomer was
still with them. They found out that no one and nothing could take from them
the life that truly mattered. And as a result, they conquered real fears as people
possessed by peace. The Spirit whom they had received was already teaching
them of their safety in Jesus.

Never was this conviction more dramatically displayed than when a man
named Stephen tangled with religious types who hadn't encountered the life of
Christ. These men didn't take too kindly to Stephen's claims. His offensiveness
resulted from a simple fact: He, like the rest, had taken the Olivet promises seriously. He, too, testified that this Lord had risen from the dead and was still with
them by His Spirit (Acts 6:5). Worse yet, Stephen was "full" of this Spirit. Imagine that!

The men Stephen offended weren't locals. Some were the tan-skinned
scribes from north of Palestine; others bore the beautiful olive complexion of
North Africa (Acts 6:8–9). Perhaps their anxiety had risen when they realized
this message just might reach their homelands.

And so they sought to nip the Jesus problem in the bud. But it proved a
frustrating experience, for "they could not stand up against his wisdom or the
Spirit by whom he spoke" (Acts 6:10).

One afternoon, these people found Stephen's wisdom particularly annoy-
ing. So the offended leaders arranged for false witnesses. They stirred a mob into
a frenzy. They grabbed Stephen and hauled him before the ruling council, and
would you believe what happened? "All who were sitting in the Sanhedrin
looked intently at Stephen, and they saw that his face was like the face of an
angel" (Acts 6:15).

Now you and I share a common shortcoming at this point: We've never
seen an angel's face (at least not knowingly). But can't you envision Stephen?
We've all seen the guilty-as-sin guy leaving the courthouse with a phony smile
plastered on his sorry face, vainly attempting to hide his guilt from the public.
And we've all seen the politician standing before the flash cameras and micro-

phones trying foolishly to portray an air of confidence when anyone with an ounce of perception could clearly see that the poor chap was in deep trouble.

Apparently, that's what these religious men expected Stephen to look like.

Apparently, that's the exact opposite of how he actually appeared.

Stephen was at peace. Confident. He was right, and he knew it. He possessed real life, the life of the Risen One. And he was safe.

How do you explain that?

The Spirit made him do it.

The High Priest asked Stephen to defend himself (never a good thing to ask a preacher). So Stephen opened his mouth, and the Olivet Promise spoke up. The life of Jesus spilled out like fine wine.

*I* wonder if Stephen knew he was delivering his last sermon. When you read it (you can find it in Acts 7:2–53), it appears that, as he approached the sermon's end, Stephen decided to go for all the marbles. I doubt that anyone other than Jesus Himself has delivered a more powerful conclusion:

> You stiff-necked people, with uncircumcised hearts and ears! You are just like your fathers: You always resist the Holy Spirit! Was there ever a prophet your fathers did not persecute? They even killed those who predicted the coming of the Righteous One. And now you have betrayed and murdered him—you who have received the law that was put into effect through angels but have not obeyed it. (Acts 7:51–53)

Stephen had never attended seminary. He didn't know a fraction of what your pastor knows about homiletics. We don't know his occupation; we only know he seemed like a good guy to wait tables at church (Acts 6:3–6).

But we know enough to explain his phenomenal life: Stephen had heard the word of truth, the gospel of his salvation. And he had believed it.

At that point in the progress of revelation, Stephen hadn't yet learned what you know: that the promised Holy Spirit had sealed him in Christ. He hadn't yet heard that the Spirit was a deposit guaranteeing his inheritance. But he did know his Jesus would never leave him. He knew his Master would never forsake him.

When his sermon produced the expected fury, "Stephen, full of the Holy Spirit, looked up to heaven and saw the glory of God, and Jesus standing at the right hand of God. 'Look,' he said, 'I see heaven open and the Son of Man standing at the right hand of God'" (Acts 7:55–56).

Jerusalem is a rocky place. Stones are readily at hand. The people's fury found easy expression. Soon palm-sized boulders took flight, and as they pummelled Stephen's chest and back and thighs—before that last one hit him on the skull and smashed it—Stephen uttered two brief prayers. I draw your attention to them because only a safe man, only a sealed man, only a confident heir would pray such things. Stephen prayed, "Lord Jesus, receive my spirit." And then, "Lord, do not hold this sin against them" (Acts 7:59–60).

Do those words sound familiar? They should, because Jesus also prayed them with His last breath (Luke 23:46, 34). Stephen was just a man. He bled and felt incomprehensible pain as the rocks struck their mark. But his mind was so full of Christ's glory that he could take pity on the poor dupes whom Satan used to kill him.

Incredible! When the life of Christ is real within us, we speak the way He did. And the words change lives. That was the whole point of Olivet.

A young man named Saul stood guard over the coats that steamy afternoon in Jerusalem. He heard Stephen's sermon, bristled with rage at the sermon's conclusion. But though he tried to cover his ears, he must have heard enough. So much so that…

- a few months later on the Damascus highway, he heard a voice from heaven and he knew it came from Stephen's Lord (Acts 9:4–5);
- he would later long to follow Stephen into Jesus' presence (Philippians 1:23); and
- he would write to believers such as Aristarchus and Epaphras and you and me, describing a Sanctuary where we are safe in the life of Christ no matter what kind of stones come our way.

The Mount of Olives casts a long shadow, so long that Jesus' promises reach right where you are.

Because of the guarantee, you too are a change agent.

Because of the Seal, words or stones or guns or calamaties can't really harm you either.

Isn't it grand to be crazy enough to believe the whole thing?

Praise be to His glorious grace!

Praise His glory!

And I say yet a third time, praise Him!

# Prayer

# To Know the Beauty of His Sanctuary
## Our Quest for the Son

*For this reason, ever since I heard about your faith in the Lord Jesus*

*and your love for all the saints, I have not stopped giving thanks for you,*

*remembering you in my prayers.*

*I keep asking that the God of our Lord Jesus Christ, the glorious Father,*

*may give you the Spirit of wisdom and revelation,*

*so that you may know him better.*

*I pray also that the eyes of your heart may be enlightened*

*in order that you may know the hope to which he has called you,*

*the riches of his glorious inheritance in the saints,*

*and his incomparably great power for us who believe.*

EPHESIANS 1:15–19

*Prayer is appreciating the incredible beauty of the Sanctuary*

*and asking for better eyes with which to enjoy it.*

*A*wkward moments inevitably invade worship services, such as when:

- the reciting first-grader runs out of memory mid-verse without a clue as to the next word or idea;
- the pastor calls on so-and-so to give her testimony, and she's nowhere in sight; or
- those occasions when the unexpected occurs—an *obvious* visitor strolling toward the pulpit, a bird flying into the sanctuary during the sermon, or a senior adult stumbling in the aisle.

I myself have caused a few awkward moments. Once our church did a Christmas musical presentation and, as pastor, I narrated. (This may have been a strategy to keep me out of the choir.) After the congregation opened the service with singing, the lights dimmed until the room was completely dark, setting the mood. At that point, I was supposed to light a single candle and read an introductory passage by candlelight. I had to perform this task surreptitiously and without delay. Well, let me tell you, that room was dark. *Really* dark. I didn't know how dark it was until I couldn't light the match. As I tried and tried, to no avail, I could hear an increasing amount of nervous shuffling and even a few giggles as the auditorium remained in utter darkness.

The audience surely considered the nighttime mood more than sufficiently established. The choir members, who knew what was *supposed* to happen, probably wished they had given the narrator part to someone with better motor skills.

After the whole performance finally concluded (yes, I did eventually manage my part), we all had a good laugh as I explained to the choir that the problem was actually very simple. After all, you can easily light a match when you turn it around and strike the proper end!

If there's an awkward moment in Sanctuary worship, we've come to it. The awkwardness doesn't arise because something has gone wrong or because someone didn't do his part. It's more a matter of timing.

We've enjoyed three grand hymns filled with eternal truth. They have led us to the pinnacle of praise. We have plenty more hymns to sing—an eternity's worth, in fact. But in the sample the Holy Spirit has written for us, He has deemed three enough for now.

So what do we do next? Should someone pronounce a benediction? Should we just file out? Does our worship end here?

The silence is awkward. Uncomfortable.

It's a perfect metaphor for the Christian life, a beautiful and honest grappling with the awkwardness of living in the Sanctuary while also living in the everyday world. It has the gear-grinding sounds of shifting from worship to witness, from belief to action.

If you or I were in charge of the program, we'd scurry about, attempting to rescue the service from the disastrous lull. "Production is flat-lining! Somebody do something!" Pathetically, we react similarly in our spiritual lives. "Awkward silence. Nothing happening. Must do something. Somebody get me a new book. Find me a Bible study or, better yet, a seminar. I need an emotional experience and quick!"

But put aside, if possible, our tendency to avoid embarrassment. Let's relax for a moment in the sovereign presence of the God who designed the Sanctuary and invited us into it. If He's truly in charge, can't we trust Him to show us what to do next?

*L*et's start over (more calmly now). Our life in Christ brings incredible spiritual wealth. *All* spiritual blessings, in fact. Jesus Christ has delivered us from Devastation. And all we possess is eternally wrapped up safely in Him. The truths of Sanctuary living, sung so eloquently for us and by us, can change our lives.

But how do we allow them to do so?

The truth is revolutionary, but how do we become revolutionized? How do we move from singing hymns in the Sanctuary to singing them at work when it's embarrassing to be identified with Jesus? How do we push the grand pearls of revelation from our hearts past the lump in our throats? How does our position in Christ relate to our daily lives of smelly laundry or spread sheets or crescent wrenches?

The apostle Paul faced the same dilemma. He confronted it when he took an order for the next tent, when he prayed in jail, when he penned his letter to the Ephesians. So how, like him, do we bridge the gap between Sanctuary life and the everyday grind that pulls us from lofty truth into the grungy problems of earth?

That's the awkward silence. That's the question at hand.

And that's the issue God doesn't avoid. Through the heart and pen of Paul, God shows us the main tool that can help us transition between life in Christ and all that seems foreign to it.

How do we proceed? What do we do next? We find the right end of the match and strike it.

We pray.

And in so doing, we discover that Sanctuary living isn't a billowy-cloud experience but part of nitty-gritty reality. In so doing, the light gradually turns on, and we find that our provisions in Christ completely change our earthly experience.

But what *kind* of prayer?

I hesitate to pose that question, for too many of us are already gun-shy about prayer. We've heard about intercessory prayer and spiritual warfare prayer and city-taking prayer. We know about adoration and confession and thanksgiving and supplication. We've read about healing prayer and the prayer of faith. We know we should pray for the missionaries but never for patience.

People have so discussed and expounded upon and theorized about prayer that sometimes I wonder if I ought to cross my legs a certain way and tilt my head just so God will *really* hear me. Sometimes the subject of prayer can confuse us so much that we're tempted to distort the doctrine of predestination, saying that since God is sovereign, prayer doesn't really change anything, so let's spare Him the ear-traffic.

*I* don't want to add another knot to the prayer tangle. And I'll tell you from the start, you're not reading the words of a great intercessor but of one slugging away in the trenches just like you.

That's why the prayer before us refreshes me. It recommends no technique.

It requires no protocol. Rather, this prayer is a simple and natural response to what we see in the Sanctuary. It looks at our wealth in Christ and says, "Wow, help us appreciate that more!" It observes the depth of life in Jesus and responds, "Help us understand that better."

Or to cast it a bit differently, this kind of prayer is the logical response of someone who revisits Bethlehem and sees God's eternal love. It's what a person naturally does after trudging up Golgotha and encountering the Deliverer. It's the spontaneous reaction to hiking up Mount Olivet and basking in the panoramic promises of guaranteed life in the Kinsman-Redeemer.

In short, this type of prayer appreciates the Sanctuary's incredible beauty and asks for better eyes with which to enjoy it.

# CHAPTER NINE

# Make Yourself at Home

*Don't miss the opportunity to ask God for what He surely delights
to give you in any situation.*

The other day I took my daughter Heather to see the doctor. Over the years, Lyn and I have done this dozens of times. Parenting and doctor visits go together.

But something happened on this occasion that sent me a signal, quiet but clear. Heather and I were sitting outside the office, waiting for our turn (note the word *our*). Then the doctor opened his door and motioned for us to come in. We rose to enter his office, but both Heather and the doctor seemed to know something I didn't. The doctor politely told me, "Why don't you wait here." Heather's body language concurred with the suggestion.

This was a first. I had always gone into the doctor's office with my girls. I had always heard the diagnosis, always asked my questions. But now, I wasn't welcome. Now, it wasn't appropriate. Because now, my daughter was thirteen years old.

I sat down, picked up a boring health magazine, and pondered the harsh realities of life. *What gives a strange man the right to be alone with my young daughter while I, her own father, sit on the other side of the door, waiting to play chauffeur?*

Then it hit me. It's a matter of roles. That doctor had earned the right to fulfill a certain role. Due to his training and character, society (and I) trusted him to examine my daughter.

Roles determine appropriateness. Because that man had graduated from medical school and passed the necessary exams, he belonged in the examining room with my girl-becoming-woman. Because I was the dad, and my little girl was growing up, I belonged in the waiting room.

My wounded spirit healed a bit as I mentally tested my line of logic. I reflected on my days as a pastor. I remembered an occasion when I went into the living room of a couple who had just lost their son in an accident. Only close family members were allowed there that night. Why did they include me, a comparative stranger? Because of my pastoral role.

Do you know your role? Discovering it reveals actions appropriate for you to take.

As we listen to the Sanctuary hymns, we discern our role. (Unlike the doctor, we didn't earn our role. God gave it to us.) We're God's children. We're in Christ. We belong in the Sanctuary. We're not visitors or tourists. We live there.

How then do we behave appropriately? Is it fitting for us to obtain God's autograph to show the folks back home? Is it right to ask for a chunk of Golgotha to display on our mantles?

That's what visitors do.

It's not what heirs do.

Heirs marvel at the incredible wealth they've received. They bask in the safety of their relationships. They delight in their adoption. They swell with pride in their Brother.

Heirs are on a quest. They want to know more, not as detached scholars but as intimate stakeholders. They possess an inquisitive spirit that naturally slides into prayer.

I have to confess that over the years I've often prayed inappropriately. I've rung the doorbell when I should have walked right in. I've politely held my hat in the entryway when I should have tossed it on the hat rack. I've sat stiffly on the couch when I should have kicked off my shoes and sat back and relaxed.

I've played the role of visitor when I should have felt at home. Can you relate?

## A Wholesome Passion for God

As we learn to fulfill our role of being at home in Christ, we instinctively know how to pray appropriately. Paul found it as natural a transition as "For this reason." In other words, because of all we have received, we pray. Because the songs of the Sanctuary have enlarged our vistas, we turn to the God who graced us with the view.

And what kind of prayer emerges like spontaneous combustion? Inquisitive prayer. Discovery prayer. Paul prayed that we might enjoy such times with God:

> I keep asking that the God of our Lord Jesus Christ, the glorious Father, may give you the Spirit of wisdom and revelation, so that you may know him better. I pray also that the eyes of your heart may be enlightened in order that you may know the hope to which he has called you, the riches of his glorious inheritance in the saints. (Ephesians 1:17–18)

Prayer is an ongoing expedition, motivated as strongly as a pirate hungry for booty, as urgently as a thirsty wayfarer in the Sahara. Our treasure is life in Jesus. Our thirst is to know God in our own situation.

Do you feel the drive, the wholesome passion for God? Sanctuary prayer holds the same passion that Jacob had when he wrestled with God and said, "I will not let you go unless you bless me" (Genesis 32:26). The phraseology of the new covenant wrestler is, "Lord, give me the Spirit of wisdom!" "Father, give me the Spirit of revelation!" "God, enlighten the eyes of my heart!"

The Christian's heart isn't pitch black. Jesus, the Light of the world, has entered our lives. We just need more light. More insight. More understanding of God and our provision in Christ.

We have a very important part to play in gaining this. We must be students of God's revelation, the Bible. We must ponder and discern. But we cannot produce more light by our efforts alone. This is a divine operation. Ultimately only God's hand controls the rheostat. He's the One who increases the light.

And so we must pray for "the Spirit of wisdom and revelation." *Revelation* means an unveiling, and we need the spiritual scales peeled from our eyes so that we can see deeper truths.

If you compare translations of Ephesians 1:17, you'll notice that some Bibles capitalize the *s* in *Spirit* while others don't. So who does the unveiling?

Should we pray for the revealing ministry of the Holy Spirit (uppercase S), or should we pray that our own spirits (lowercase s) will understand more? I don't know which Paul had in mind when he wrote verse 17. If I could ask him today whether I should pray for the revealing ministry of the Spirit or for my own spirit to better understand, my guess is that he'd reply, "Yes." That is, both are true. In fact, we can't have one without the other:

> For who among men knows the thoughts of a man except the man's spirit within him? In the same way no one knows the thoughts of God except the Spirit of God. We have not received the spirit of the world but the Spirit who is from God, that we may understand what God has freely given us. (1 Corinthians 2:11–12)

When the electricity suddenly goes off in your house, how do you react? If you're working at a computer, you probably ask yourself, "Did I save my work?" If it's evening, you likely wonder where you've stowed the flashlight, candles, and matches. If you don't have a regular place for these items, you learn a good lesson in the value of light. Stumbling over end tables, bumping into corners, identifying drawer items by braille, you learn to love light.

To a degree, all of us need a bit more light. We see dimly. We know some of the Sanctuary's glories, yet many remain unknown. And so we crave insight, praying that the eyes of our heart may be enlightened (Ephesians 1:18).

You've heard of missing persons. Have you ever thought about missing prayers, prayer requests that God ought to hear regularly but that we scarcely speak? The prayer for spiritual discovery ought frequently to grace our lips.

Paul prayed for it often. As we've already seen, he prayed that the Ephesians might experience it (Ephesians 1:17). He also prayed it for the Philippians: "And this is my prayer: that your love may abound more and more *in knowledge and depth of insight*" (Philippians 1:9, emphasis mine). The Colossian church had the same need, and so Paul wrote to them: "For this reason, since the day we heard about you, we have not stopped praying for you and *asking God to fill you with the knowledge of his will through all spiritual wisdom and understanding*" (Colossians 1:9, emphasis mine). And to his friend Philemon he wrote, "I pray that you may be active in sharing your faith, so that you will have a *full understanding of every good thing we have in Christ"* (Philemon 6, emphasis mine).

Such prayer turns our focus from what we want to what we really need: God. It admits our helplessness and acknowledges the Source of help. It confesses shallowness and pleads for the depths.

> *God, help us pray the missing prayer*
>    *and change our errant focus,*
> *from this or that we want to get,*
>    *to understanding Jesus.*
> *Forgive us, Lord, for prideful prayers*
>    *that falsely boast of fullness*
> *when, truth be known, our hearts are dim.*
>    *We're groping for the matches!*

## As the Light Grows

When we have an electrical blackout at our house in Nairobi, the whole family knows exactly what to do. (This has come from a fair amount of practice.) We light the lantern. It's a small, inexpensive, kerosene lantern. Nothing fancy, but exactly the prescription for a dim house.

And I'm glad we have it, because when the lights go out in our house, I notice that I suddenly feel lonely. I know my wife and daughters are there; I can hear their voices. But only when one of us lights the lantern do I *see* them. Only then can I sigh with relief, "Ah, that's better."

Let's be honest: Sometimes our hearts grow dim as well. Our stances on issues are undefined, like furniture in the dark. We have difficulty making out Jesus' face. And when my heart grows dim, I feel lonely. God doesn't seem close. I think I have to solve all my problems by myself, that I have to clear up my confusion without help. And I don't know exactly how to pray.

Gradually, I'm learning what to do when my heart-light goes dim. I start praying for the things I *know* God wants to give me, such as wisdom, understanding, faith. I pray that He will be glorified in the situation, that He will accomplish His purposes. In short, I pray for spiritual qualities rather than circumstantial changes. This helps me take a different approach to God and prayer. It goes something like this:

1. As we receive the spirit of wisdom and revelation (from the only Spirit who can give it to us), we gain the wisdom to know what pleases God and the eyes to see as God sees.
2. When we gradually learn what pleases God and begin to see as He sees, we start to naturally pray as He wants us to pray.
3. Since we progressively pray more as God wants us to pray, we're less selfish in what we ask for and more confident that God is pleased to grant our requests.

May I take us back to Olivet for a minute? Remember that vineyard we discussed? On the way through the Kidron Valley, Jesus talked to His disciples about staying connected to Him. He said if they played the branch and allowed Him to be the vine, they'd be fruitful. Then He touched on the subject of prayer: "If you remain in me and my words remain in you, ask whatever you wish, and it will be given you" (John 15:7).

The first half of that verse provides a wonderful definition of Sanctuary living: We abide in Him, and His words abide in us. When we do that, our viewpoint changes. The light comes on. We see what truly matters, and we begin to pray in line with the eternal riches God has already determined to give us.

God loves to answer His own requests!

## "If it Be Thy Will"

Sometimes we ask God for help or healing and feel constrained to add "if it be Your will." This isn't necessarily bad. Rather than showing a lack of faith as some might chide, this phrase can indicate a submission to God's sovereignty and a desire to pray according to His will.

Still, wouldn't it be wonderful to feel confident enough to omit that "*if*" from our prayers? To *know* that we're praying according to God's will? Scripture depicts such prayer as highly desirable: "This is the confidence we have in approaching God: that if we ask anything according to his will, he hears us. And if we know that he hears us—whatever we ask—we know that we have what we asked of him" (1 John 5:14–15).

*W*hen we pray to receive wisdom and revelation from God, when we ask God to light the lantern of our hearts, there's no need for saying, "If it be Your will." There's no "if" about it! We know God will answer that prayer affirmatively.

Praying such a prayer is like a son asking his father to teach him to be more responsible or a daughter requesting her mother to teach her about better planning. Mom and Dad long to teach these lessons, to convey such insights to their children. Parents (if they don't faint first) don't think twice before saying, "Of course I will!"

Too often we pray with a predetermined outcome in mind. Don't misunderstand me: God wants to know our desires. We ought to express them. But we shouldn't miss the opportunity to ask God for what He surely delights to give us in any situation. A few examples:

> "Lord, you know I'm in a real crisis at work. Help me to know Your peace as I respond to the accusations. Help me to understand my security in You even if I lose my job."

> "I'm depressed today, God. Don't even feel like praying. Would You at least let me know You're with me today? Thank You for Your love and grace, even though I don't feel them."

> "Father, Ralph is very sick. May he come to know You more deeply through this trial. Allow him to feel the safety which is rightfully his in Christ, even while enduring scary times."

See the recurring theme? Instead of "Please solve this problem, God, by doing A, B, and C," these prayers say, "Show me Your perspective on this problem, and help me love You more as I go through it."

Maybe that kind of prayer seems boring. ("Where's the flair and faith in that?") And I'm not saying we shouldn't make detailed requests of God. But I think that from heaven's perspective, the prayers above score a "10." God doesn't have to think twice about what to do. He delights in answering yes to prayers that affirm the desires He already holds for us.

When you dwell in the Sanctuary, you're not a visitor. You can kick off your shoes, pull up a pillow, and settle in. You're at home. The host is your Father, and you know exactly what He wants to give you.

No ifs about it.

*Dear God,*

*A radical thought just hit me.*

*The Old Testament prophets used to pose questions such as*

*"Who can understand God?" and "Who can fathom His ways?"*

*The obvious answer is that no one can.*

*But I'm beginning to realize that I need to keep trying.*

*Need to seek understanding.*

*Thank You for the Sanctuary—*

*where I can know more about You than I ever thought possible.*

# CHAPTER TEN

# As Big As God

*Coming to know God will take an eternity.*
*We'd better start now and keep asking.*

Ever hear of a "sucker pitch"? If you haven't, don't feel stupid or somehow deprived. It's just the term we used on my boyhood baseball diamonds as third-string batters with Mickey Mantle dreams.

A pitcher never wanted to throw a sucker pitch, and a hitter always hoped for one: a medium-paced toss right across the middle of the plate. A sucker pitch usually resulted in a new number on the scoreboard (and often a new pitcher on the mound).

One day, John the Baptist's disciples went through their windup motion and collectively threw their leader a juicy sucker pitch. They said, "Rabbi, that man who was with you on the other side of the Jordan [Jesus]—the one you testified about—well, he is baptizing, and everyone is going to him" (John 3:26).

Hey, you in the bleacher seats, get out your mitts. It's home-run time! The time when the campaigning politician steps to the podium and says, "I know you've all heard that my opponent is popular down on the south side, but don't be fooled." When the CEO writes the memo that leads the charge into the fray, vowing bigger sales and huge profits. When the preacher (I'm skating on thin ice here) with the largest congregation in town sanctimoniously inquires about a neighboring (and obviously smaller) church, "What are they running on a Sunday morning?"

Sucker pitch!

I wish you didn't know your Bible so well (not really), because I can't even surprise you with John the Baptist's response. I can't tell you what he actually said and have you exclaim, "Incredible!"

You know his reply because it's the most famous one-liner of his life: "He must become greater; I must become less" (John 3:30). Or perhaps the sound bite you've heard is from the New American Standard translation: "He must increase, but I must decrease."

Connecting with a sucker pitch and sending it on a one-way safari over the fence is incredibly gratifying. It feels good. It brings cheers. It humiliates the other guy. And John could have gratified himself by solidifying his followers' loyalty. He could have said, "Jesus can do what he wants, but look at the throngs that come to hear *me.*"

But John was a much greater man than that. You know why he was great? Because he knew his role and he played it. John knew that as great as he might be, there was One even greater. So John played his part. He deferred to greatness.

I'm convinced that as we pray, we constantly impede our progress because we're forever getting in God's way. While He's trying to take center stage, we're out there doing some ridiculous tap dance. We're supposed to decrease, but instead we assert our needs and desires, our plans and agendas. Consequently, our prayers stay as small as our requests. What could be grandiose remains puny.

Sanctuary prayer remedies intercessory smallness. It removes us from the limelight and allows God to move onstage where He belongs. He must increase, while we must decrease.

Wouldn't you like to learn how to pray this way? (Now there's a sucker pitch for you to hit out of the park!)

## How to Survive a Windstorm

Recently, I drove down a road I travel every day from work to home. A long row of huge trees, majestic and tall, line that road. As I drove that particular day, I couldn't help but notice that, where once a huge tree had stood, a clump of roots jutted toward the street. During the night, the wind had blown over that mammoth tree. One glance revealed the reason: whereas the tree had stood about one hundred feet high, the protruding roots measured only about ten feet long.

Many of our prayers reveal our impression of towering spiritual growth. We ask to know God's will for our lives. We ask which job to accept, which courses to take. We ask for health and finances. We pray that our bodies will heal, that our churches will grow, that our children will obey. We stand against injustice, we bemoan immorality. And as we do, the trunk reaches skyward and the branches widen like stretching arms.

And this is good. We need entire forests of these trees, grown by great prayers.

But I'm still bothered by those roots I saw the other day. Because they were shallow, the beautiful tree with lush green branches had crashed perilously close to an apartment building.

A principle is at work here. When the winds come, trunks can flex and branches can bend. But trees ultimately withstand storms because of the strength of their roots.

What sinks spiritual roots deeper and deeper into the soil? Prayers of the Sanctuary. Prayers for understanding and insight, prayers to know and love God better. A deep-rooted intimacy with God helps us survive the storms.

But most people don't pay attention to roots until a storm comes. (When you look at a beautiful grove of trees, how often do you ponder, "Are the roots healthy?") When a hurricane rips through our lives and leaves us clutching for an anchor in the wind, we wonder what happened to our moorings. We marvel at how shallow our roots are.

The apostle Paul wrote to churches that were young saplings sure to confront strong winds. And so he prayed for them the way we need to pray for one another and for ourselves. For clarity's sake, let's strip away a few words to understand the essence of his prayer for the Ephesians: "For this reason…I keep asking…that you may know him better (…and to do this, you'll need the Spirit of wisdom and revelation)." Or try this personalized paraphrase: "Because of all these Sanctuary blessings…let's keep praying that we may know Him better."

Knowing God! There are many wonders in the human experience, but none is more enthralling than the possibility of knowing our Creator. We can confide in Him. Worship Him. Ask His counsel. Request His strength. Desire His wisdom. All of these lie at our disposal from the Creator God.

But how does this happen?

Reflect for a moment on what has drawn you close to your best friend. How did you reach a level of intimacy with that person?

*O*ne way we can become close to friends is by sharing intense and extended experiences with them. Go on a camping trip with another person or couple, and I won't have to spend any more words illustrating this concept. An experience such as a shared weekend, tenting, cooking and cleaning, and sitting by a roaring campfire can advance a relationship by quantum leaps. (It could also bring the curtain down on a fledgling friendship!)

You can sit around and talk, sharing stories of your childhood or courtship. You can share the struggles you have raising children or your challenges at work. You can learn who likes to cook and who can build a good fire. (On one such camping trip, I was supposed to bring the firewood, which I did. Unfortunately, I couldn't find any *dry* firewood. We struggled the whole weekend to make a decent fire. We mainly produced smoke and sizzle. Derogatory references to "Bob Logs" hounded me for months afterward.)

On a deeper level, extended time together can uncover unmet longings and deep motivations. Friendship can move past acquaintance to heart companionship, past the "How are you? I'm fine" niceties to the "I'm actually struggling" realities. Intense experiences expose qualities that rarely surface in routine living. You know a friendship is growing when occasionally you say, "As long as I've known you, I never knew you thought that way!"

Not to overdo the camping analogy, but we earlier likened the Sanctuary to a tent in which God has placed all spiritual blessings. And there's no better way to get to know God than to spend extended time with Him in the tent, working, enjoying, exploring.

I was rummaging around the Sanctuary one day, and as sometimes happens, I discovered a familiar truth as if for the first time. It was the fact that because I'm "in Christ," Jesus' Father is my Father. This may seem simplistic, but my heart responded deeply to this thought, perhaps because my relationship with my human father has been one of the most significant and emotional connections of my life. As I pondered this dimension of my inheritance, I jotted down these thoughts:

It is the practice of every saint to say "Heavenly Father." But there are few who come to cry out, "Oh, Abba!" When one's heart is so filled with the privilege of sonship—when he is lost in the glory and beauty of his relationship with the Father, when he cannot contain the depths of wonder—he cries out that which somehow expresses the inexpressible: "Oh, Abba!" May I have the heart of a wise son, a heart that yearns to please his Father always. When a son's heart yearns for his Father, the presence of that Father is ever near, even if a great distance separates them. The son never lives out from under the influence of the Father—His wisdom and instruction are always felt. Wise and blessed is the son whose heart is possessed by his Father.

My meditative "campout" in the life of Christ produced a greater knowledge of God. Through it, I discovered one of the provisions of my life in Christ, one which has often strengthened me since.

Think of how enriched our lives will become as we spend a lifetime exploring, by prayer, "every spiritual blessing in the heavenly places in Christ"! Think of the improved view we'll have of ourselves and of our value to God! And think of the eagerness that can develop within us to keep on learning! A. W. Tozer was obviously in the tent when he prayed:

O God, I have tasted Thy goodness, and it has both satisfied me and made me thirsty for more. I am painfully conscious of my need of further grace. I am ashamed of my lack of desire. O God, the Triune God, I want to want Thee; I long to be filled with longing; I thirst to be made more thirsty still. Show me Thy glory, I pray Thee, so that I may know Thee indeed. Begin in mercy a new work of love within me. Say to my soul "Rise up, my love, my fair one, and come away." Then give me grace to rise and follow Thee up from this misty lowland where I have wandered so long. In Jesus' Name, Amen.[1]

Prayer is our best way to join the twelve disciples and walk with Jesus. Granted, we can't serve the Lord a plate of vegetables and beef stew. Can't wash His tunic for Him or prepare Him a cot in the guest room. But are we truly that disadvantaged? What would the disciples have done after licking the last of the beef broth from their lips? What would they have done before showing Jesus to His cot? Wouldn't they talk with Him? Wouldn't they ask Him to explain things over again? Wouldn't they express appreciation for some truth they had learned while the cabbage rose to a boil?

The essence of Sanctuary prayer is a dialog between the disciple and the Master: "Lord, could you go over that one more time?" "God, could you help me see that more clearly?" No ruffles or frills. It's a simple desire to "know him better."

## Asking Wisely

Childhood can be baffling. Take the matter of requesting something from parents. The child asks for it, and Mom or Dad says, "No you can't, and please don't ask for that again," or "Sure you can. You may ask for that whenever you want."

What's a kid to do?

If the child is smart, he or she will become a student of Mom and Dad's wishes and learn the skill of successful asking.

As a parent, I have the responsibility to deny my children certain requests. If one of my daughters came to me and asked, "May I drop out of high school?" I would withhold permission. Why? Because I know that dropping out of school isn't in her best interest.

On the other hand, I could endure repeated requests for any number of other desires. Allow me to indulge myself with a few examples:

- "Dad, could I sweep up the walkway?"
- "Dad, could we spend some time together tomorrow? I need to discuss a problem."
- "Dad, could I borrow your Bible commentary?" (Okay, so I stepped over the line from reality to fantasy on that one.)

Get the idea? What parent wouldn't gladly field these kinds of requests many times over? Why? Because we love our children and delight to grant them that which is good for them.

But what if a child fails to distinguish between the "ask once" questions and the "keep on asking" questions? The child will experience two unfortunate results. First, he will grow frustrated. In asking again and again for that which the parent won't grant, the child will encounter a string of refusals.

Second, if the child doesn't keep on asking when she should, she will miss out on some beautiful gifts. Let's say that I, as a parent, want to grant my teenage daughter the gift of adult responsibility. I know she needs this, and I want her to have it. Let's also say that my daughter wants to be trusted to do more adult-like things. So one day she approaches me and says, "Dad, I'd like you to give me the responsibility of an adult."

I think to myself, *This is a wonderful request. I want to grant it.* So what do I do? Do I say, "I give you permission to go out this afternoon and find a job, get married if you want, buy a house, move to another city, write a will, purchase a car, save for your retirement, become pregnant, raise children, care for your aging parents, and start your own company"? All of these are positive answers to my daughter's request for adult responsibility. And I may want all of these for her.

But I would be foolish to give them all to her in one sentence. Why? Because some gifts are so big that the receiver cannot handle them all at once. And therefore, the child needs to continually ask for the gifts so the parent can grant them in appropriate amounts.

That's the way it is with our quest to know God better. And that's why Paul says, "I keep asking." Just as my daughter learns to carry adult responsibility one step at a time, you and I come to know God better bit by bit. We explore the Sanctuary room by room. One insight builds on another, until gradually, throughout our whole lives, we have a better understanding of our Father and the blessings He has stored up for us in the heavenly places in Christ.[2]

Coming to know God will take an eternity. We'd better start now and keep asking.

When John the Baptist resisted the temptation to clobber the sucker pitch, he set a high standard for us to emulate. Sucker pitches cross our strike zones every hour—delectable invitations to gratify ourselves and humiliate the other guy.

Even in prayer, temptations to focus on ourselves abound. And plenty of coaches eagerly encourage intercessory selfishness. They tell us to ask for what we want, to seek a prize in a kind of faith tug-of-war with God. Such prayer fronts as godly belief in God's bigness but often disguises an ungodly failure to surrender to His purposes. It falls short of recognizing that we can know God and that sometimes suffering and sickness is the straightest path to such knowledge.

There's a better way. It's saying to God, "May You increase, and may I decrease."

That's prayer as big as God.

*God, can You see underground?*

*I'm not referring to the underground of ants and gophers.*

*I mean the soil of my soul. I'm wondering how deep my roots are.*

*Wondering if I'll be able to withstand the next storm.*

*What if the big one hits? Will I make it?*

*This I know: I want to make it.*

*I want roots so deep in You*

*that roaring gales will pass over me like soft breezes.*

*So I'm asking once again, and I'll keep on asking, to know You better.*

*Please help me persist. Protect me from selfish distractions.*

*Drive my roots into the bedrock of Your strength.*

# CHAPTER ELEVEN

# Three Journeys

*True Christian prayer must have theology in it; no less than true theology must have prayer in it and must be capable of being prayed...Prayer and theology must interpenetrate to keep each other great, and wide, and mighty.*

P. T. Forsyth[1]

Visiting a gold mine is an unforgettable journey. On a sunny afternoon, I had the privilege of leaving the world I knew and traveling to one I had never before seen. It lay below the sprawling city of Johannesburg, South Africa.

The experience left me with several deep impressions (excuse the pun):

- the incredible volume of manpower required to carve the massive subterranean labyrinth of shafts and corridors;
- the mind-boggling accomplishment of the engineers who succeeded in building a megacity underground, fully equipped with waterways, electric supply, and transport systems all running like clockwork;
- the immeasurable cost in human life created by the grinding poverty of the indigenous population and the insatiable lust for wealth by those who held the power of opportunity and technology; and
- the immense wealth that God made all the more precious by hiding it in flecks and nuggets in the obtuse creases of the earth, a silent metaphor of the value of seeking until finding.

Emerging from the wire-cage elevator after a couple hours in this underworld, I felt like I had been to another dimension and back. I had visited a realm that had existed all along but had lain undiscovered.

Today we will launch a journey—journeys, actually—far richer in discovery and life-change than the world's deepest, richest gold mine. We're going to take journeys you can't reach in an elevator. We'll uncover booty better than the finest gold, and find a world that God engineered.

The Sanctuary.

When I went into the gold mine, I had to qualify. For example, I needed to be a certain age. I needed the entrance fee. I needed the desire and courage. I needed the time.

Once I qualified, I needed some preparation. Those in charge told me what to expect. They told me to stay with my group. They put a lighted helmet on my head and a battery pack on my waist.

Journeying into the Sanctuary also requires certain qualifications, and not a little preparation. If you've sung the hymns, you know the requirements. You also know that if you have Jesus Christ, you meet all the qualifications and you're totally prepared. He's the entrance fee and the elevator. He's the gold mine and the gold. He's the world yet to be discovered.

Previously, we traveled outside the Sanctuary and witnessed devastation wrought by the lion. Now we have the privilege of traveling into the life of Christ to enjoy the wondrous beauty to be found there. Our first trip was dark and left us nauseous. This one is brilliant and encouraging, granting us joy.

A bit of orientation before we leave: This journey will turn into three. We'll not linger for long on any one of them, but each glimpse will stay with us for quite a while.

So let's begin. This journey always starts simply, with plain words. If you think this is a childlike way to initiate such a memorable trip, you're right, for the words are, "Dear Heavenly Father...."

## Journey to Hope

*"That you may know the hope to which he has called you."*

Picture a student. She has worked hard through high school to earn good grades. She has fixed her sights on a good college. She and her parents have applied for a scholarship. Without the financial help, she won't be able to realize her dream. So now they wait. Each day when the mail arrives, the search ensues. "Did it come?" has become the family greeting.

Or picture a lone man on a frozen lake. He has cut a hole in the ice. Huddling by a simple shelter, warmed only by an occasional cup of lukewarm coffee from his thermos, the fisherman looks steadfastly at the line extended into the water. He shivers but persists.

Finally, picture a young woman. She stands at the arrival gate at the airport. She continually checks her watch. She glances every minute or so at the doorway through which the passengers will emerge. She straightens her dress and tidies her hair. She waits anxiously but joyfully, for she hasn't seen her fiancé in weeks.

Some people would look at the mailbox and see only letters. They would look at the hole in the ice and see a cold reason to go home. And they might wait at an airport and just see a bunch of people.

But these three are not just some people. These are people of hope. Hope sees a scholarship in that mailbox. Hope envisions a fish dinner. Hope can already feel a loving hug.

I doubt if we could live long without hope. Of course we could keep our hearts beating and lungs breathing. But I'm talking about *living!*

Devastation distinguished itself by the complete absence of hope, worsened by fear. Entrance into the Sanctuary has brought abundant hope, strengthened by love. Jesus gained the scholarship, He caught the fish, He insured the beloved's safe arrival.

He created us to be a people of hope. And hope permeates the Sanctuary. It flows through us. As we are aware of our life in Christ, we gain more than enough hope to help us wait through any situation.

The problem is that we who are "in Christ" often live like we're still out in the lion's muck. We fearfully dread his pounce. We act like we have no hope, no God.

Have you given up? Do you figure you've waited long enough, prayed often enough? Have you concluded that you've apologized frequently enough, failed more than enough?

A brief query: Who told you to quit? Did the Lord tell you to throw in the towel? Or have you just lost hope, lost sight of the goal?

If so, Jesus is calling to you today. Calling you back to hope. Calling you to the riches of the Sanctuary.

*God of hope, I seek You today.*
*Deliver me from this hopelessness.*
*My blood is flowing but my heart has stopped living.*
*Turn on the lantern of my life, that I may see You again.*

(Say, didn't that fishing line just twitch?)

## Journey to Glory

*"The riches of his glorious inheritance in the saints."*

You're keeping very good company these days. In fact, you're three peas in a pod:

- "glorious grace" (Ephesians 1:6);
- "glorious Father" (Ephesians 1:17); and
- "glorious inheritance" (Ephesians 1:18).

As I say, excellent companions. The grace of God, the very person of God, and you.

*What do you mean?*

The inheritance. That's *you.* Not only have you received an inheritance, but the saints are *God's* inheritance. He delights in them like glorious wealth.

*I'm sure the saints are very happy about that.*

Look at the Father's pride. Look at the Son's happiness regarding them. And the Spirit fills each and every one with joy and peace!

*I'm tickled for them. Guess they're pretty special, huh?*

Yes and no.

*They're saints because of some special feat such as martyrdom, aren't they? Or they're revered for great wisdom.*

No, they're special because they're holy.

*Right, that's what I mean. They're holy, not like us normal folk.*

These saints are holy, not because they've produced holiness but because they've received it.

*I wish I were like them.*

You are.

*No, I'm not. I don't feel the way they feel.*
But look at yourself. You glow just like they do.
*Wrong. I don't feel any glow.*
God looks at you with the same pride and joy as all the rest.
*No kidding?*

*Lord, peel the scales from my eyes that I might see myself as You see me.*
*I feel the exact opposite of a saint. If I'm Your inheritance, You got*
*gypped—at least in my view.*
*Help me see that I'm valuable to You.*
*Chosen. Adopted. Redeemed. Sealed.*
*Loved.*

## Journey to Power

*"And his incomparably great power for us who believe."*

We now embark on the third journey, and I suppose by now you realize these aren't trips to places as much as steps to understanding. Wisdom and revelation are our vehicles, their Spirit our guide.

Now He takes us to a place where a man sits at his expansive desk, placed prominently against the full-length windows of his sprawling office. The dark blue of his three-piece suit contrasts powerfully with the distinguished graying of his temples. The immaculately starched shirts hanging in the closet stand at attention, waiting their turn to march into yet another boardroom and fill the chair at the head of the table.

Who is this man? Oh, just someone. One of a million rich people who play power games.

Maybe he's powerful because he's the main shareholder in a huge conglomerate. Maybe he commands respect as the chief benefactor of a global charity. Or perhaps he wields influence as a substantial financier of a major political party.

But for a moment, let's talk about power. A kind of might has been unleashed in this world that shakes heaven's rafters. Stronger that prison steel, it can set captives free. Mightier than the bastions of science, it can make the lame walk.

The power of which I speak is greater than boardroom takeovers, more valuable than any stock market bonanza. For this power can make enemies walk together as friends, can cause armies to lay down their weapons. It can restore husbands to sobriety, can transform egotists into caring parents.

What would it cost to have this kind of power? What would the man with the starched shirts give to control this kind of influence?

I'll tell you what he *ought* to give. His own soul.

But even that isn't necessary. Look at the people who wield this greater power. See that elderly woman kneeling by her nightstand. And look at that fellow in his cramped office, reading the Bible as he munches his tuna sandwich. Notice that teenage boy in the hallway at school and that homemaker in the kitchen at home, praying for him to make the right choices.

These are people of the greater power.

These are the believers.

*God, thank You for placing a force within me*
*that the world will never understand.*
*Help me explore Your power*
*and understand when and how You would like to unleash it.*

## To New Depths

Having glimpsed the parts of our journey, let's now put it back together as a whole. Paul wrote:

> I keep asking that the God of our Lord Jesus Christ, the glorious Father, may give you the Spirit of wisdom and revelation, so that you may know him better. I pray also that the eyes of your heart may be enlightened in order that you may know the hope to which he has called you, the riches of his glorious inheritance in the saints, and his incomparably great power for us who believe. (Ephesians 1:17–19)

Seems logical, doesn't it? When we enter the Sanctuary, we find it natural to pray as Paul did.

The *requests* make sense: for the Spirit of wisdom and revelation, that the eyes of our hearts may be enlightened. Who else but God can take us on the spiritual explorations we crave?

The *goal* makes sense: to know Him better. Who else but God offers a worthy pursuit for our spirits?

And the *journeys* make sense, too. They reveal who we are as Sanctuary dwellers:

- We are called—recipients of His choice;
- We are saints—conveyors of His holiness; and
- We are believers—responders to His truth.

Each part of our identity in Jesus Christ carries with it a corresponding spiritual reality:

- We have hope—blessed with a bright future;
- We have glory—inherited by a loving Father; and
- We have power—energized by a mighty God.

I doubt if any kind of prayer can delight God more than this. There's probably nothing better for our souls, either. So let's refuse to return to banal prayers for shallow requests. Let's press on to the far reaches of our life in Christ. It just makes sense.

When I visited that gold mine in South Africa, the elevator ride down the mine shaft seemed to take three or four minutes. Granted, we weren't descending at breakneck speed, but we weren't crawling at a snail's pace either. After finally reaching the bottom, we walked and walked through low passageways, viewing different kinds of cutting techniques and support structures.

A salty old Afrikaner served as our guide. He had delivered his spiel many times before and had finely tuned his jokes. We laughed politely on cue. (Given our location, we wanted to stay on his good side.)

Finally, we arrived at the end of the corridor. Our guide brought the group to a halt and cleared his throat. "This is a map of the mine," he said, motioning toward an antique engineer's drawing fastened to the wall. "Can anyone tell me where we are in the mine?" Our guide's personality reminded me of an elementary school teacher who ridiculed anyone who offered the wrong answer, so no one in our group came forward very enthusiastically. But one overachiever in the front (who obviously hadn't gone to my elementary school) suggested we must be somewhere near the very bottom. I nodded inwardly; I was sure we were.

Our guide smirked ever so slightly. I could tell this stop was a highlight of his tour. "We are right here," he boomed with gleeful voice. And as he did so, he pointed to the *top* of the map, to the shaft nearest the surface! We had penetrated only a fraction of the mine, like a toothpick in a forest, like a drop of water in the Pacific. The guide told us that if we could stretch all the mines under Johannesburg end to end, they would reach all the way to Cape Town (an eighteen-hour drive by car).

I'm mighty glad Jesus doesn't use the map technique! It would be humbling to realize that we have only *begun* to explore the depths of our life in Christ, only begun to apply His resources and blessings to our daily living.

The point is obvious, isn't it? The kind of prayers we typically pray won't get us very far in the amazing depths of the Sanctuary. To fully realize what God has provided, we must start taking prayer journeys, the kind Paul shows us: the journey to hope, the journey to glory, the journey to power in Christ Jesus.

And it probably goes without saying that the three trips we've considered aren't at all exhaustive. They're just a beginning. For the terrain of Sanctuary prayer is as vast as the infinite character of our Savior.

*Dear Lord,*

*thank You for those times when the elevator*

*has taken me deep into my wealth in Christ.*

I've needed and enjoyed that close fellowship with You.

You've guided me through difficult times, and You've given me the thrill of

drawing near to You.

But I seem to get stuck periodically.

Even tend to surface, forgetting my need for You.

My pride swells my head and presses the "Up" button.

Please put the lamp of truth on my head and draw me beyond my familiar

boundaries, to new regions of faith and understanding.

O God, give me an explorer's heart!

# Amen!

Amen (Greek): *"so let it be, truly, amen," a liturgical formula, at the end of the liturgy, spoken by the congregation; a particle beginning a solemn declaration, "truly, truly."*

It was one of those turbulent ministry transitions. Jesus had ascended the mount with Peter, James, and John and had been "transfigured" before them. God's voice had thundered from heaven. God's glory had shown up.

But even Jesus didn't live perpetually on the mountaintop. So down they traveled. And what they found was a mess. They arrived to discover a confused mob, nine frustrated disciples, and a bungled deliverance. A man in the crowd offered the explanation:

Teacher, I brought you my son, who is possessed by a spirit that has robbed him of speech. Whenever it seizes him, it throws him to the ground. He foams at the mouth, gnashes his teeth and becomes rigid. I asked your disciples to drive out the spirit, but they could not. (Mark 9:17–18)

There are two sentences I would hate to hear from the Lord's mouth (and to be honest, I deserve them both). One of them is, "Could you not keep watch for one hour?" (Mark 14:37), which Jesus said to His groggy disciples in the Garden of Gethsemane.

The other sentence I would not want to hear from Jesus is the one He said to the disciples after descending from His transfiguration, after they failed to overcome the evil spirit that was plaguing the poor lad. He said, "How long shall I put up with you?" (Mark 9:19).

If I had been one of those disciples, I would have found no less than a million tufts of lint I needed to pick off my tunic immediately. My sandal would have needed tying, my neck would have needed rubbing, my cell phone would have needed answering. *Anything* would have proven an adequate reason to avoid eye contact and escape the brunt of those words!

Well, the Lord dealt with the evil spirit and freed the boy. Then Jesus entered someone's house, and the disciples slinked in after Him. (No need to open the front door. They were so low they probably crawled right under it!) I have to give them credit for attempting to tie the loose ends that had unraveled. "Why couldn't we drive it out?" they asked Him (Mark 9:28).

Jesus' reply brings us right to the heart of the issue at hand. He said, "This kind can come out only by prayer" (Mark 9:29).

You probably understand that we don't always know Jesus' exact words. In this instance, some manuscripts record "only by prayer," others have "only by prayer and fasting." But let's not miss the larger point. By either rendering, what did Jesus *mean?* Did He say, in effect, "Fellows, you forgot to open the deliverance with a word of prayer"? Did He mean, "Guys, you failed to recruit a team of intercessors to pray during the confrontation"? Was His point, "If you had skipped breakfast you would have had more spiritual gumption"?

No. These may be important prayer activities, but Jesus had something different, something bigger in mind. Jesus was taking the disciples beyond the *wording* of prayer, even beyond the *fervency* of prayer (as evidenced by something such as fasting).

Instead, the Master was emphasizing the *lifestyle* of prayer. In essence, He told the disciples, "You can only meet this kind of tough challenge successfully if you know the value of prayer and show it by your prayerfulness." Jesus overcame the demon because He communed often with His Father. Moment by moment, in fact. As a way of life, He drew on heaven's power.

*W*hile there are indeed some words I would hate to hear from my Lord, there are also some words I would love to hear. Right now I'm thinking of one word in particular. I'll bet you'd love to hear it, too. We'd love to hear it as He looks over our shoulder in prayer, love to hear it as He intercedes along with our feeble requests.

We would love to hear Him say, "Amen."

And He would love to see a new resolve in your heart and mine right now, a new desire to deeply explore the Sanctuary in prayer. He'd love to find a renewed commitment to lingering in His presence, to soaking up the hope of heaven, the glory of belonging, the power of faith. He'd love to cheer us along, love to say "Amen!"

So let it be.

# Doxology

# Praise for His Trail of Triumph
## Our Victory in the Son

That power is like the working of his mighty strength,

which he exerted in Christ when he raised him from the dead

and seated him at his right hand in the heavenly realms,

far above all rule and authority, power and dominion,

and every title that can be given,

not only in the present age but also in the one to come.

And God placed all things under his feet

and appointed him to be head over everything for the church,

which is his body,

the fullness of him who fills everything in every way.

EPHESIANS 1:19–23

Praise erupts when we realize

that our Savior conquered the summit

and that He didn't conquer it alone.

*I*f you look directly at the sun on a clear day, you won't look for long. You'll take more of a blink than an outright look. Some things are just too brilliant to stare at. In these cases, it's better to look at the periphery and thereby gain a feeling for the core.

I guess that's why I'm often intrigued by the "side events" of the Golgotha weekend. When I look directly into the glare of the crucifixion and resurrection, the eyes of my heart can stand only so much. I can't take it all in. But if I look to the side, I feel the power of the center.

Take, for example, the events that took place near Golgotha. Matthew lists them like a journalist short on space:

At that moment the curtain of the temple was torn in two from top to bottom. The earth shook and the rocks split. The tombs broke open and the bodies of many holy people who had died were raised to life. They came out of the tombs, and after Jesus' resurrection they went into the holy city and appeared to many people. (Matthew 27:51–53)

Can't you just see those priests on Mount Moriah tending to their temple chores? In an instant, an unseen spiritual knife cut in half the curtain that took months to sew. You can almost hear their collective, *"Oy vey!"*

Throughout Jerusalem, the earth trembled. Rocks split. Some of those rocks had been carved for tombs, and the now-liberated tenants marched to see if their wills had been properly executed.

Staring at Golgotha might hurt your eyes, but an indirect glance allows you to feel the power anyway. And what's true for Friday works on Resurrection Sunday, too. Again, Matthew is on the scene:

There was a violent earthquake, for an angel of the Lord came down from heaven and, going to the tomb, rolled back the stone and sat on it. His appearance was like lightning, and his clothes were white as snow. The guards were so afraid of him that they shook and became like dead men. (Matthew 28:2–4)

If you've ever experienced a major earthquake, as I have, you know that more than the ground trembles. Earthquakes also shatter nerves! Pity those Jerusalemites. They had a horrendously confusing day on Friday, and the ground shook again with a violent earthquake on Sunday.

Though the guards were bribed to keep it under wraps (Matthew 28:11–15), word probably leaked out that what caused the sunrise commotion was the landing of a radiant angel who had a stern disagreement with a huge tombstone.

The final scene of this sideshow is of the Roman guards, the finest of the fine, handpicked for this most important assignment, keeling over as dead men under the angel of the Lord's piercing gaze. What price we would have paid for front row seats at *that* episode!

All of these events were observed by people whose sandals rested firmly on dirt. These people were historical eyewitnesses. They felt the earth shake. They saw the rocks split and fall. They heard the frightening sounds of granite grinding underground. They heard resurrection reports from those who had attended their own funerals.

*B*ut the Holy Spirit wants in on the celebration, too. He witnessed other events that also demand reporting. And to deliver His testimony to us, He requires that we look up from the earthly phenomena to take in the heavenly dimension. In effect, He wants to touch our eyes with the strength to look at the brilliant core of Christ's victory.

Earthquakes and angels are amazing to behold. But the Spirit knows that they are damp matches compared to the fireworks on the heavenly side of the tomb. That's why the Holy Spirit, praying through the apostle in Ephesians 1, comes to the word *power* and launches Paul's intercession into the orbit of doxology.

And He proceeds to teach us that when we live and worship in the Sanctuary, we had best become accustomed to bending our knees before our awesome and powerful God. Better get used to raising our hands in glad acknowledgment of His awesomeness.

And we should also become accustomed to having that same power at our disposal, because we who believe are part of the story.

Jesus climbed the tortuous hill and triumphed. He mastered the peak.

But hold on. There's more. The incredible news is that He wasn't alone when He did it. You and I went with Him!

And that's the stuff of which doxologies are made.

# CHAPTER TWELVE

# God the Showman

*When the Father energized Christ to ascend above all others,*
*He power-charged the Sanctuary in which you and I live.*

The day following Jesus' death was the Sabbath, the day of rest. Ironic. For although Jesus' body rested in the grave, the formidable grip of death worked overtime, clutching Him with desperate tenacity. Jesus had succumbed to the tomb, but would He stay there?

At the same time, the pecking order of the heavenlies maintained a kind of mock truce. More like a fragile cease-fire. The stronger demons had seized control of their elevated positions. The weaker, resigned for the moment to their lower estate, plotted future maneuvers. But for now, the evil spirits felt relieved that the Main Threat was behind stone.

Who were these revelers in the status quo? Paul describes them as "rule and authority, power and dominion" (Ephesians 1:21). A *rule* is a domain based on prior existence.[1] On burial day, spirits gripped high positions in the heavenlies because they had claimed them for centuries, if not millennia.

Then there were *authorities*.[2] In the spirit realm, they had the legal right to act. They had warrant to throw their weight around. Some had a lot of clout and were proud of it.

Some held their rank based on *power*.[3] These were perhaps the militant sorts, drawing on raw spiritual force to shove others around.

*Dominion* was the claim of other spirits.[4] Little lords they were. Or not so little.

Still others stood behind the power of their *titles*.[5] Names are more than identifying nomenclatures. They represent strength and authority. Many spirits speak their names and enjoy the superiority they instantly convey.

With the Threat locked away in the earth, the future for these beasts of evil looked beautifully dark, not just for this age but also for the ages to come. ("Forget those stick-on name tags, fellas. Bring out the permanent name plates!") Everyone was happy with the status quo.

Everyone, that is, except God the Showman.

Theirs had been a pathetic four-part harmony. A sweatshop quartet, sung in minor key. Status quo meant more Gregorian-like monotony.

Then suddenly, from the silent tomb of stone came a single ear-splitting voice like twelve trumpets in perfect harmony. The fanfare crescendoed until it drowned out every other competing melody.

The Showman couldn't pass up *this* audience. The cocky confidence of evil lordships and self-important titles had to be shattered. And God shattered them when He lifted mighty arms and wrenched His Son from the grip of death. Like a confident conductor signaling his choir to stand, God raised His Son to the cheers of angels.

No wonder the doxology celebrates this moment! "That power is like the working of his mighty strength, which he exerted in Christ when he raised him from the dead" (Ephesians 1:19–20). The word *exerted* is the Greek word *energeo*. Sound familiar? The Father energized the Son, empowering Him for the most incredible triumph ever. And in so doing, He infused the Sanctuary with power beyond comprehension. He took authority over the so-called authorities. He overpowered the would-be powers.

## Trail of Triumph

Jesus once told a parable of a dinner guest (Luke 14:7–11). In this story, He referred to the pecking order at many such parties. Hosts in that day designated certain seats for important guests and others for no-names.

In Jesus' story, a guy walked into the dining room of a big wedding reception and surveyed the seating arrangement. *Plenty of bleacher seats left. Oh, look over there—a box seat just for me!* And so he decided to go for the gusto. He chose the best seat in the house, probably at the head table with the nicest centerpiece and fanciest silverware. The works.

Then, according to the parable, the host approached the head table and, upon seeing this "nobody" in the guest-of-honor's seat, promptly bumped him to the peanut gallery.

I'm sure Jesus had everyone smiling at that point in the story. We smile too. (Aren't you smiling a bit inside?) We smile because we've all experienced embarrassment and, at times, have done something equally as presumptuous as that seat-grabber.

When Jesus had the people smiling, He knew He had achieved a teachable moment. So He told the folks that it would be much wiser to enter the banquet hall and sit in the *lowest* place available. To be sure, they would risk the chance of spending the entire evening in that low seat, unnoticed. But, said Jesus, the host just might spot them and, stricken with incredulity at such a breach of propriety, make his way through the crowd, take them by the arm, and announce to everyone that people of their stature absolutely must sit at the table with the splendid centerpiece!

At this point, you might wonder what this parable has to do with our doxology. Let me explain.

As I thought about what happened to Jesus during His life, this parable came to mind. In a way, Jesus was the wise guest in the story. He scoped out the available positions in life and chose the lowest one. He humbled Himself. Then the one in charge said, "Come up here and sit by me."

Trace the promotion in the Sanctuary doxology: "He raised him from the dead and seated him at his right hand in the heavenly realms, far above all rule and authority, power and dominion, and every title that can be given, not only in the present age but also in the one to come" (Ephesians 1:20–21).

First, Jesus was *dead.* He voluntarily opted for the lowest position. Remember who He was: "Who, being in very nature God, did not consider equality with God something to be grasped" (Philippians 2:6). That is, He deserved the best silverware and the padded chair with the high back. Jesus was God. Yet He chose the wooden bench with splinters: "But made himself nothing, taking the very nature of a servant, being made in human likeness. And being found in appearance as a man, he humbled himself and became obedient to death—even death on a cross!" (Philippians 2:7–8).

Dead. Lifeless. Kaput.

But the parable isn't over, and neither is the doxology. Note the next section of the promotion trail. Jesus was *raised from death*. This is not mystical transformation. No spiritual migration of the soul. This is a guy in a coffin of stone, arising and dusting off the flakes of cellular decomposition. This is the Host approaching the Guest of Honor sitting in the bleacher seats and saying, "You deserve better than this! Arise, and come with me."

Where does the trail culminate? The doxology sings out the glorious answer: "And seated him at his right hand in the heavenly realms" (Ephesians 1:20). That's right. Jesus was *seated at the place of honor*. He's now at the head table "far above all rule and authority." Not just slightly above. Far above.

> Therefore God exalted him to the highest place and gave him the name that is above every name, that at the name of Jesus every knee should bow, in heaven and on earth and under the earth, and every tongue confess that Jesus Christ is Lord, to the glory of God the Father. (Philippians 2:9–11)

People sit down in various ways. There's the flop on the couch after a long day's work. There's the polite and formal placement of the posterior on the dining room chair belonging to someone you want to impress. There's the disinterested dropping of a sacklike carcass into the back row of chemistry class. There's the eager sitting-on-the-edge-of-your-row-A-seat, front and center on opening night of a big play.

Lots of different ways to sit down.

Jesus Christ sat down. I wonder how He did it.

How would *you* sit down at the right hand of God? Well, if you were Jesus, you wouldn't be nervous, for you've earned the seat. You wouldn't feel out of place, for God has reserved the seat for you, and no one else can fill it.

I think Jesus sat down like the King He was. He sat regally.

And all his subjects emitted a sigh of relief.

And all the defeated rulers, authorities, powers, and dominions threw their name badges in the trash can.

## The Power of the Name

Let me call him Patrick. He was a missionary and a good one. Dedicated. Helpful.

And defeated.

For many years, Patrick had been enslaved to sexual lust. I had the privilege of coming alongside him for a whole year, offering prayer and accountability. I cheered him on when he made it through a month without stumbling. But Patrick fought a fierce battle. He occasionally slipped into sin, and when he left his country of service to return home, the fight still raged within him.

It would be comfortable to believe that Christians always live in victory. It would also be fake. Truth is, our enemy is vicious, and our fleshly nature is not well-behaved. The two make for a deadly combination.

I believe you probably understand what I mean. I don't need to ask you any piercing questions. You know the struggle, as do I. May I interest you, therefore, in a little discussion about the name of Jesus Christ?

If you served the Allied Forces in North Africa during World War II and heard that Rommel was coming, you'd get a shiver up your spine and place yourself on instant alert. Or if you had enlisted in the Japanese military during the same time period and heard the news that MacArthur was on the way, you'd listen for your plan of action and wouldn't miss a word of the instructions. Why? Because in the context of battle, a name signifies power, rank, and authority.

It's no different in the fight you now fight. When Paul says that Jesus Christ has been elevated to a position where His name is far above any other, it means that throughout the entire spirit world no name signifies more power. No other name carries a higher rank. The demons—even the most powerful princes of darkness including Satan himself—know they're outranked by Jesus Christ. They know that the instant they hear Jesus' name, they're overpowered and underequipped. Their hearts must sink immediately, for they know they have no hope of winning—Jesus Christ has already gained the heavenly position to win ultimate victory, and in fact has already dealt the strategic blows of defeat in His temptation, crucifixion, resurrection, and ascension.

Consider the implications. When the believer prays and uses Jesus Christ's name with faith and aggressiveness, shock waves of disappointment must run through the ranks of the satanic forces. Evil spirits and powers cower and hide because they know that as the praying saint persists, they will soon be weakened, debilitated, and sent away in humiliation.

Of course, it isn't the praying person who causes such chaos among the evil spirits and wreaks havoc with their wicked plans and strategies. Rather, when the praying person uses the strongest name in the universe, evil hasn't a chance. Jesus Christ has given us His name as our greatest weapon. With it, we bring to our local battle all the strength of the largest and most crushing army in the universe.

And we don't have to worry about how long Jesus will manage to hold on to His present strength. His dominance over all applies "not only in the present age but also in the one to come" (Ephesians 1:21). It's no spiritual tug-of-war that either side could win. Jesus' place as King of the heavenly realms is permanent and unthreatened. No one could ever successfully mount a coup. Christ's name is preeminent and will remain that way forever. He is the eternal Sovereign.

The demonic hosts must find this the most discouraging realization. They have no hope of turning the tables. They must know that their subjugation under Jesus' feet is permanent. Their defeat is assured, yet they mechanically fight on, stupidly delighting in an occasional skirmish won. They take encouragement in minor victories, trying to ignore the hard reality that their master, Satan, has lost miserably. He foolishly rebelled, and the demons idiotically followed his lost cause. And now they're trapped in eternal defeat and damnation. The die is cast.

The permanency of Christ's victory has powerful significance for humans. While we live, we still have the choice to either follow Christ or rebel against Him. We must reckon with the seriousness of our choice, for the consequences are eternal. Since Jesus' name will be all powerful in the age to come, a decision to reject Him will prove permanent and irrevocable. A person who has made such a choice has no hope beyond the grave, for a lost person will forever be Christ's enemy.

How can I adequately stress the finality of Christ's power? Being with Him and sharing His victory is eternal triumph and rejoicing. But opposing Him or even ignoring Him means joining Satan's defeated kingdom and enduring the misery of separation from God—in every age and eon to come. The most sobering choice a person must make is how he or she will spend the great unending.

Those of us who have chosen Him still face the challenge of the present battle. And while we live in the strength of our Victor's powerful name, using His authority to resist temptation is no easy task guaranteeing automatic results. Just ask my friend Patrick.

But fight we must.

*L*et's back up for a moment. Do you recall how we discovered this doxology? We were foraging around in the gold mine of the Sanctuary's wealth. In one of our prayer journeys, we came across His "incomparably great power," at which point the Holy Spirit indulged Himself by giving us a grand reminder of the whys and wherefores of might. We'll benefit from backtracking at this time to emphasize four crucial words about the power. The power is great, yes. Incomparably great, in fact. But notice this. It is incomparably great power *for us who believe!*

When the Father energized Christ to ascend above all others, He power-charged the Sanctuary in which you and I live. And now we face the challenge of living and fighting in this earthly battle using the rank and authority of our heavenly Commander. With feet touching earth, our hearts must draw strength from heaven. While our eyes see people and cars and trees, we must train our souls to see our Master at the head table:

- "Fix your thoughts on Jesus, the apostle and high priest whom we confess" (Hebrews 3:1);
- "Set your hearts on things above, where Christ is seated at the right hand of God" (Colossians 3:1).

"Fix your thoughts." "Set your hearts." That's where the struggle rages, where we must experience the supercharged Sanctuary of Christ's life.

Do you want to be a revolutionary? Do you want to undertake the battle that spans heaven and earth? Do you want to be changed? Set free?

The battlefield is right there in your mind and heart.

And the winning strategy is to live your earthly reality in light of His heavenly victory.

*Lord Jesus, I'd be a fool to pretend to understand Your humility.*

*Deserving the best, You chose the lowest place.*

*But thank You.*

*Thank You for rolling up Your sleeves and becoming involved in my world.*

*And thanks for finishing well.*

*Your name is my call to arms. It's my strategy, my weapon.*

*You are my Commander, and I don't ever want to lose sight of You.*

# CHAPTER THIRTEEN

# Tilt the Mirror

*We, the Church, are God's plan for this age
and His delight for the age to come.*

If you're one of the few and proud who have achieved Christian nirvana—some self-defined state of perfect and sinless bliss—you can close this volume early and loan it to a lower life-form, because in the next few pages I'll be talking to mere mortals such as myself. Bye.

(Okay, is it just us now?)

I vote for a little honesty. Truth is, the Christian faith is no panacea for happiness, and it never promised to be. We who follow Christ have just as many trials as those who ignore Him. In fact, I sometimes wonder if we're not ahead on the suffering scorecard.

The brothers and sisters who preach that Christians have no excuse for ever feeling depressed ought to quit using amphetamines as throat lozenges. And folks who say they haven't experienced temptation in months ought to experiment with something other than cryogenics.

I find it easier to relate to the guy who prayed, "Lord, so far my day is going really well. I haven't felt envious of anyone. Haven't been grouchy with my wife. Haven't even yelled at the kids. But Lord, I'll be getting out of bed in a few minutes, and I'm really going to need Your help then!"

I'm sorry, but I sometimes feel discouraged and haven't a clue as to why. I've confessed all the sins I know about. I've yielded my life to the Holy Spirit. I've played praise tapes…and I'm still down in the dumps.

I tell God I want to be a holy man. I want thoughts so pure they squeak. When a fetching woman walks by in clothing two sizes too small, I want eyes that look straight into elsewhere. But alas, my eyes sometimes go AWOL (absent without leave), and my thoughts lose traction and slide into the mud. (There, I think I've adequately descended from my pedestal. Transparency is a virtue to which I aspire. I don't want you to think that I live in defeat, but I'm concerned that we churchgoers tend to feign righteousness too often.)

So now that we're here on ground level, let's talk. How do we deal with sin? What help does the Sanctuary offer us in our ongoing battle with our flesh? Plenty.

I need to ask you to use your imagination again. Picture a mirror in which you see the full-length image of the Lord Jesus. (I don't care what He looks like. He could have a beard, a goatee, or a clean shave with a new blade. He could wear sandals or cowboy boots on His feet or a tunic or denim work shirt on His torso. Point is, you're looking at Jesus.) Now, over His chest, envision three big words in capital letters:

- DEAD
- RAISED
- SEATED

Unless you went on a long vacation since reading the last chapter, you'll recognize these three words as the three steps in Christ's "trail of triumph." God supercharged Jesus and has seated Him at the head table in the heavenly places, far above every competitor. Forever.

Stay with me. In your Bible, at the end of Ephesians 1 you'll see a big number *2*. Yes, it indicates the beginning of a new chapter, but it also denotes something much more. Pretend the page is a mirror and that, right at the chapter marker, the mirror folds in half from top to bottom. When you tilt the lower half of the mirror toward the upper half, you see a double image.

Here's the reflection you'll see when you tilt the mirror at chapter 2:

But because of his great love for us, God, who is rich in mercy, made us alive with Christ even when we were *dead* in transgressions—it is by grace you have been saved. And God *raised* us up with Christ and *seated* us with him in the heavenly realms in Christ Jesus. (Ephesians 2:4–6, emphasis mine)

Forgive me if this mirror illustration seems corny, but I want to indelibly imprint a thought in our minds. In the Sanctuary doxology, we've already seen the image of Jesus with three words emblazoned across His body: DEAD, RAISED, SEATED (Ephesians 1:20). Now, as we read further, we see an exact reflection of Christ in ourselves as believers. When we tilt the mirror, we see that we who are in the Sanctuary have walked the same trail of triumph as our Savior:

- We too were DEAD—in our transgressions (Ephesians 2:1, 5);
- We too were made alive (Ephesians 2:5) and RAISED with Christ (Ephesians 2:6); and
- We too were SEATED with Him in the heavenly realms (Ephesians 2:6).

The one who believes in Christ for salvation is the spitting image of Jesus. There you are, side by side with Him in the matching mirrors. Jesus was dead because of crucifixion. You were dead in your sins. Jesus was raised from the tomb. You were raised from spiritual death to eternal life. Jesus was seated at the right hand of the Father in heaven. So were you, because you are "in Christ Jesus." You're in the Sanctuary.

A simple grammatical tool of the Greek language expresses this shared triumph. During Paul's era, if you spoke Greek and wanted to turn the word *go* into the phrase *go together*, you simply added the prefix *sun* (pronounced "soon") in front of the word *go*. Guess what Paul did in Ephesians 2:5–6? He added *sun* to three words. The result? God "made us alive together," He "raised us together," and He "seated us together" with Christ.[1]

One more mind-blower. Paul didn't write these verbs in the future tense. He wrote them in the *past* tense. These three actions have already happened...to every believer. Through His gift of the Sanctuary, the Father has already accomplished these deeds.

If I ask you "Where are you?" you have a two-fold answer. Bodily, you are on planet Earth. But in another way you're already in the heavenlies, with and in Christ. Your position, your belonging, your citizenship, your inheritance are all at God's right hand right now! That means you've ascended above the evil echelons. You have more authority in Christ than the wicked authorities. You have Christ's power, which is more than the evil powers possess.

The trail of triumph is the spiritual route you have *already* taken in Christ. And it is the route *you will take bodily* as soon as God releases you from your temporary housing of skin and bones.

## Declare the Truth

Meanwhile, we wait. And fight the fight. We yearn to dwell in the heavenlies, but we accept our assignment to stay on earth and live for Him.

God is intimately aware of how tough that is. That's why He has told us so clearly about our life in Christ. Anytime we need a reminder of our resurrection from spiritual death, we simply have to tilt the mirror. It's not a trick mirror but the *truth* mirror of God's Word. When we see Christ's image on one side and ourselves on the other, we need to believe what we see: We've conquered the trail with Christ. Then we need to go out and live that way. As Paul said, "In the same way, count yourselves dead to sin but alive to God in Christ Jesus" (Romans 6:11).[2]

When your eyes go AWOL, when your heart cheats on you, declare truth in the face of falsehood. Call it...

### MY NEW CREED
I, _____, was dead in my sins
*but because God loves me and has been rich in mercy toward me,
I am alive together with Christ.
I've been saved by grace.
God has raised me up with Christ
and has seated me with Him in the heavenly realms
far above all rule and authority, power and dominion,
not only in this age, but also in the one to come.*

I believe we need to be transparent about our struggles as Christians. Phony idealism won't impress anyone except those content to play games. But I also believe we needn't be fatalistic. We have hope. We have a way out. We have already won the war.

The next time you feel depressed, unloved, worthless, or overwhelmed by the lie that you don't really matter, tilt the mirror. Whenever you face temptation or give in to it, whenever you feel powerless to do what is right or feel dirty because you didn't, tilt the mirror. If you hear accusations in your mind that you're a no-good wretch, that you're vile to the core, that God doesn't really love you, tilt that mirror of truth. You're seated with Christ in the heavenly places. God has raised you with Him. You don't have to be a slave to sin any longer (Romans 6:5–14).

Look at your resemblance to Him. Striking, isn't it? Both of you were dead. Both were raised. Both were seated. Forget the peanut gallery. You're sitting in the big chair with the velvet cushions. You're in Christ!

## The Apple of God's Eye

The pendulum of human craving is currently swinging back toward spirituality. Folks have laid down their bets on the acquisition of knowledge, the stockpiling of wealth, and hope in education and have come away from the table with empty pockets.

So many are turning once again to the arena of faith. They cry for connectedness with others on the spiritual plane. Human spirits long to be in touch with higher forces in creation. This is good, for it's a move in the right direction.

If you're seeking spiritual reality, hang on to your beads and bandannas. Crystals and karmas beware, you're about to tread on holy ground!

We've discussed how God's power has transformed people so that their souls mirror Christ's cosmic ascent to the summit of the heavens. Now let's follow the ancient Scriptures one step further. Can you imagine the collective force of millions of such people, all connected to this same Lord, all infused with the same eternal power? Can you fathom a huge host from every nation and people on earth who have already been vested in the eternal plan called redemption?

Try. Because right under our noses exists the most amazing spiritual phenomenon in the history of the world. This revelation of which I speak isn't really new, but it's high time we contemplated it in a fresh way. It's an entity saddled with more preconceptions and misdirections than the oldest horse in the barn. You've probably tried it out, worn it out, and possibly spit it out. Yet it persists as the apple of God's eye.

I refer to the people of God, the Church.

Most of us view life individualistically. We sing "No Man Is an Island," but truth be known, we see ourselves as just that. I have news for you. The Sanctuary confronts island-living. It connects us with others who also follow Christ. This might surprise you, but the three hymns, the prayer, and the doxology of the Sanctuary have not once referred to Christians as individuals. Check me out. The words include *us* and *we*. And when Paul says "you," he always uses it in the plural form. Literal translations forthcoming...

- *you all* were included in Christ (Ephesians 1:13);
- *you all* were marked in him with a seal (Ephesians 1:13);
- I have not stopped giving thanks for *you all* (Ephesians 1:16); and
- so that *you all* may know him better (Ephesians 1:17).

I rechecked every *you* between Ephesians 1:3 and 2:10. All plurals.

Folks (or should I say "y'all"?), we believers are in this Sanctuary together! Our experience in Christ is just the same. We are the Church, Christ's body. And God is mighty proud of us. In fact, take a deep breath for the doxology's climax: "And God placed all things under his feet and appointed him to be head over everything for the church, which is his body, the fullness of him who fills everything in every way" (Ephesians 1:22–23).

God's Spirit once again draws our eyes from the periphery to the hot core (try not to blink): All things are subservient to Christ. He is head over everything. He fills everything in every way!

We've come to expect huge words to describe Jesus. But we find it shocking to read magnanimous words about God's view of *us*. We find it difficult to fathom that we who follow Christ are "his body, the fullness of him who fills everything in every way."

Christ lacks nothing. He's not a half-filled glass. Yet in some inexplicable way, the Church "tops off" Jesus Christ. God has designed it such that true believers form the earthly complement of our heavenly Head. Jesus doesn't *need* us, but He favors us with the privilege of being His reflection. As we mirror His triumphant trail, we amplify His glory. We are His fullness.

Some of us have a pretty dilapidated view of the Church. It has burned us or abandoned us, bored us or accused us. Who needs it? But we adopt that perspective when we see the Church as merely an organization or a denomination, when we view the Church as nothing more than a band of folks who follow a human leader, produce budgets, and build buildings.

But our doxology doesn't praise the programs or personalities or physical buildings of local churches. It exalts the Church itself, the Body of Christ. We can busy ourselves every day and night in church programs and still miss out on the Church. We can have titles and degrees in religion, can have the vocabulary and clout of church leadership, and have absolutely no clue what the Body of Christ really is.

What is the Church? It's Jesus' life expressing itself fully in and through a group of believers. It's that body of people who share with their Head the experiences of death, resurrection, and enthronement in the heavenly places.

For many, even some believers, the Church has become just one more reference book on a long, full shelf. It's one source to consult, one factor of many to keep in mind. But we contradict ourselves when we're favorable toward Jesus and noncommittal toward His body. Refusal to participate in the full expression of His ascendancy is spiritual decapitation.

Sanctuary dwellers, whether accountants or students or homemakers or bank presidents or pastors, are Church people by their very calling. Each has received a spiritual gift. Why? For their own benefit? No. To build up the Church (Ephesians 4:12; 1 Corinthians 12:7).

Christ expresses His love and power around the world through those who, by faith, are "in Him." He fills this body of saints with His own fullness. How could it please Him when we take the Church lightly, when we leave it on the periphery of our lives, midway down our list of commitments?

We live our membership in Christ's body through our involvement in one of its earthly manifestations, a local church that honors Jesus. On the scales of eternity, belonging to a local expression of Christ's body (even with all its organizational tangles and personality quirks) is still simply the most wonderful privilege afforded to any person—more honorable than election to Congress or Parliament, more regal than inclusion in a royal family, and more prestigious than controlling a Fortune 500 company.

Friend, our Head bends the knee to no one. It's time for His body to stand up and be counted. With feet firmly planted in the struggles of earth and eyes fixed on our heavenly hope, we, the Church, are His plan for this age and His delight for the age to come.

*I can think of nothing greater than to be in Christ.*

*No greater trail to climb than to be dead to sin,*

*raised to new life, and seated in the heavenly places . . . with You!*

*God, I will never return to defeated living.*

*We, Your Church, will not go back. We are bullish on the Church.*

*We are ecclesiastical optimists!*

*And when tempted to falter, we will tilt the mirror*

*and see our victory in Christ.*

# Hallelujah!

**Hallelujah (Hebrew):** *"Praise the Lord;" it occurs as a short doxology in the Psalms, either at the beginning or at the end, as in Psalms 104 and 105. In the New Testament, it is found in Revelation 19:1, 3, 4, and 6 as the keynote of the song of the heavenly multitude.*

A month ago, our family took a drive along the main road in Nairobi. We approached one of the busiest and largest traffic circles in the city center: four lanes of traffic, all in a hurry. A gap appeared in the traffic, giving us an opportunity to enter the flow. And then we saw it, the most unexpected visitor to a whirling roundabout. We all gasped simultaneously. Motionless, alone, and kneeling helplessly between lanes of traffic was a terrified, palm-sized kitten!

Lyn emitted a heart-sinking cry: "Oh, no. She's going to be crushed." Indeed, in just seconds a car or truck would most certainly and inadvertently flatten the gold-and-white kitty.

Before I knew it, we had flowed with traffic past the kitten. "We have to save her," someone exclaimed. But there's one thing you never do in a busy roundabout: You never stop!

Yet this was a helpless kitten. So I decided to round the circle to see if the kitty was still alive. She was. I slowed down, pulled up alongside her, and did the ridiculous: I stopped, positioning our pickup so the kitten was just underneath my door. I opened it and reached down to pick up the cat. Terrified, she squirted from my grasp and darted beneath our truck.

Cars and trucks had screeched to a halt behind us. One huge eighteen-wheeler found itself blocked by my little quarter-ton. Drivers were unhappy. Horns honked in ignorance of the intense drama.

Lyn jumped from our vehicle and peered underneath, but she couldn't find the kitten anywhere. An African man who had watched the scene came over and told us that the kitty had jumped up into the wheel well. He reached up and succeeded in pulling out the frightened creature. Lyn brought the kitten into our truck and we sped off, releasing the anxious flow of traffic once again.

Our hearts were racing. The kitten was petrified. But she was safe.

Over the course of these pages, we've traced a common thread: God's unrelenting determination to rescue a people for Himself and place them safely in the Sanctuary called Jesus. He has given us every possible blessing. He has emptied out the heavenly treasure chest and lavished us with grace goodies.

He has chosen us as objects of His love. He has adopted us into His family. He has sealed us permanently in His safe care. He has drawn us close by giving us the gift of prayer, and He has raised us up with Christ and seated us in the heavenlies.

We're safe in His Sanctuary. Hallelujah!

But one question remains. Will we accept all that God wants to give us? Will we lay down our pride and self-sufficiency and humbly receive all that God has provided for us in the Sanctuary?

I ask this for a reason. We're not unlike frightened kittens. We often find it difficult to trust that there's someone who doesn't mean us harm.

Lyn appropriately named the kitten Roundabout. When we brought her into our home—a chore because the poor petrified creature climbed under the dashboard and wouldn't budge—she couldn't receive our love. An eye infection had clouded her vision, and she hissed and spit at any moving object. She cried throughout those first nights, and though Lyn rose many times to give her food and comfort, Roundabout wouldn't settle down. She feared affection.

Contemplating this situation later, Lyn journaled her thoughts:

One night as I was holding her against her will, stroking her under the chin, her eyes closed in total pleasure, it struck me: This is how Jesus feels with us at times. We are poor, hungry, blind, and naked. He wants so much to take us in, abused as we are, and tenderly nurse us back to health. He longs to love us, to comfort us, but we hiss and spit at Him instead. Only rarely do we allow ourselves to be cuddled and petted.

We're too afraid of losing our "freedom," and our fear separates us from His gentle loving arms. I wept as I realized I had done the same thing to Jesus that my kitten had done to me. Fear had kept me from my Savior's tender care. My scrappy roundabout kitten made me realize that I, too, could be carried and comforted by a Shepherd longing to do so, if only I would trust Him. Thank You, God, for the reminder that Your love is constant, no matter how abused or battered we may be.

*T*he patient tenderness of my wife and daughters paid off. They applied medicine to the kitten's infected eyes until she healed. They fed her and petted her. And in just a week, Roundabout was playing with a little ball, jumping, and chasing her own tail.

Friend, when you feel abandoned, when it seems you're in a four-lane traffic circle and a truck is just about to run you down, remember: There's a safe haven. And there's Someone who wants to love you there.

# Group

# Discussion

# Guide

The following discussion questions are intended for use with small groups. They do not review the material in the chapters but seek to help group members apply the chapters to their own experiences.

The questions are only suggestive and may be complemented by others the leader considers helpful to the group. An atmosphere of acceptance and trust within the group will help members to share more openly. We also suggest that you conclude each discussion with a time of prayer for one another—specifically, prayer that God would enable each group member to personally appropriate His wonderful provisions of the Sanctuary.

# CHAPTER ONE

## Refugees Like Us

1. Do you have an early recollection of a time when you were at risk? Can you think of a time when you were really lost? If so, describe this time.

2. In a similar way, can you recall a time when you felt really safe? If so, what made you feel so safe?

3. Do you currently feel at risk in any way? If so, what kinds of deliverance would provide a safe haven from that risk?

4. Do you agree that we have a refugee problem in the Church? Why or why not? If so, what expressions of this problem do you observe? In what ways do you feel like a refugee yourself?

5. Reread Ephesians 1:3–6. As you do, picture God as a divine Father. What is the tone, feeling, or personality you perceive about that Father? How is this consistent with or different from your prior thoughts about God?

6. What obstacles do we need to overcome if we are to believe that God has prepared a tent called Jesus and has stocked it full of wonderful gifts for us?

# CHAPTER TWO

# The Rightful Owner

1. Have you ever experienced the satisfaction of rightfully owning something? If so, why was it such a good feeling to own that item?

2. How do our internal voices sometimes try to persuade us that we as Christians don't rightfully own all spiritual blessings?

3. How do you react to the fact that God chose you to be His, just as He chose Mary to give birth to Jesus? Does it give you reassurance, cause you to feel unworthy, or both? Explain.

4. God chose His children before the foundation of the world, which means our inclusion in God's family cannot be based on our performance but on God's decision to favor us. In what ways can this truth

make a difference in our everyday lives (similar to Bob's "bad day" experience and the Nairobi team's planning day)? Give some specific examples.

5. How do you react to the idea that God has brought you into the Sanctuary to make you holy and blameless? What are some ways we can better cooperate with Him in this effort?

6. In the closing prayer, we admit that we've often thought of ourselves as "unspecial." What are other secret names we tend to give ourselves? What new names would God like us to use for ourselves?

# CHAPTER THREE

# *The Highlight of His Day*

1.  What's the first thing that pops into your mind when you hear the word *adoption?* How have you developed your impression of adoption? (If any group members have in any way participated in an adoption process, invite them to share their experiences.)

2.  The Bible says that God has adopted Christians into His family. Does this stir up any special feelings in you? If so, what do you feel?

3.  Discuss the teaching that God has placed the Spirit of His Son within us to help us experience the reality of our adoption. Can you detect any ways in which that Spirit sometimes makes you yearn for your "Abba, Father"?

4. Bob characterizes adopted children in three ways: (1) They are born in adverse circumstances; (2) They face an uphill climb; and (3) They are brought into the adoptive family by an extraordinary string of miracles, producing a unique kind of love. Do you identify with these three experiences in either your physical or spiritual life? If so, how?

5. Since adoption is one of the gifts God has placed in the Sanctuary for us, let's explore some of the blessings that accompany it. Read Romans 8:15–17 and Galatians 4:4–7. What are all the benefits we possess because of our adoption?

6. Every person who truly believes in Christ for salvation has also been chosen by God and adopted into His family. Based on that fact, how should we view and act toward each other as Christians?

7. What are the implications for those not yet following Christ? Does the idea of spiritual adoption mean that those people are not chosen and therefore cannot ever come to know the Lord? Why or why not?

# CHAPTER FOUR

*Devastation*

1. What are your general reactions to the journey outside the Sanctuary? Was it hard to envision, or quite easy? Why?

2. What are your thoughts about the words from the lion's mouth: "I can kill you anytime I want, and there is no telling how terrible death will be. Nothing could be worse. And who knows what will come after that. This is all you have. Cling to the now. You see it and know it. It's safe. This is as good as it gets"?

3. Satan delights in destroying families, as illustrated in the debilitated woman's story. How does Satan repeat the same schemes in families today? How has he attacked your family recently?

4.  Read 2 Corinthians 4:3. Have you ever been prevented from seeing the truth? If so, how? Do you agree with the idea that those wearing such blindfolds cooperate with the blindness? Why or why not?

5.  The story of the princess rising from her casket is a sobering one. Do you agree with Bob's conclusion that no one would heed her appeal? Why or why not? Why would people reject such a warning?

# CHAPTER FIVE

*But God Roars Louder*

1. Have you ever felt trapped or held captive? If so, would you be willing to share your story?

2. Redemption is a "setting free by payment of a ransom." Bob asserts that Jesus releases captives as a guerrilla soldier and as a healer restoring sight to human hearts. As you consider Jesus setting you free in such ways, how do you feel?

3. Read Proverbs 18:10. Do you need to run into the strong, safe tower of the Lord right now? If so, why? What has He promised to provide when you do so?

4. Speaking of the biblical truth that believers are completely forgiven in Christ (Romans 8:1), Bob wrote, "If we could just begin to appropriate

this incredible truth into our daily lives, we would be revolutionized. ...Our families would change. We might not even recognize our churches!" In what ways do you think a better understanding of this truth would revolutionize our lives? Our families? Our churches?

5. What are the key elements in beginning and maintaining a freedom to be "crummy people who have received complete acceptance from Christ and from one another"?

6. The young Muslim man searched for the truth and God rewarded him with understanding. What is the status of your own searching for truth? How is God responding to your level of search?

# CHAPTER SIX

# It'll All Add Up Just Fine

1. A person's future can blow up in his or her face through a difficult experience such as loss of a job or child. A future can also seem to dissipate because of depression or lack of opportunity. Has the future ever looked so bleak to you? Would you be willing to explain the circumstances and the outcome? How does your future look to you at the present time?

2. This chapter describes the Sanctuary's peaceful atmosphere due to Christ's calm character. How should that serenity transfer to we who are "in Christ"? What are the obstacles to enjoying that peace?

3. Have you ever felt that God was late in unfolding His plans for your life? As you look back, can you see why waiting was actually the best thing for you, or does the waiting still seem to have served no purpose? Explain.

4. It requires a great deal of faith to believe that "all the random factors of human history will be totaled up, and the sum will be Jesus Christ." Do you find this truth difficult to believe? Comforting to the soul? Both? Explain.

5. How do you feel realizing that there may always be mystery about God's ways, even in heaven? Explain.

6. Bob discussed how ingenuity often rises from poverty. What examples of that have you seen in your travels or in your own personal experiences? What ingenious work would you love for God to do in your life and family?

# CHAPTER SEVEN

# Safe and Sound

1. Have you ever had an experience similar to Barb Butler's, where you felt the comforting presence of Christ amid dangerous circumstances?

2. Growing up, did you feel emotionally safe at home? Why or why not?

3. How do you feel about the fact that our world holds real danger, even for Christians? Explain.

4. All the potential insecurity of our lives does not weaken our safety and sealing in Christ, our Sanctuary. How can you apply this fact to your own situation?

5. The results of feeling unsafe are fear and worry. How have you been doing in the worry category? How can others pray for you so you can believe that, when you dwell in the Sanctuary, no one can really harm you?

# CHAPTER EIGHT

## Your Rustproof Inheritance

1. Has the concept of inheritance lost importance in society today? If so, how and why?

2. Consider your moral inheritance. What life values have you received from your parents?

3. When God planned your inheritance, He decided it based on generosity. As you read through the vaults of your inheritance, which one(s) bring you the greatest delight?

4. The Holy Spirit serves as a deposit, guaranteeing the full realization of our inheritance. Meanwhile, we live with the frustrations of sick bodies, unholy minds, and a godless society. What frustrations ("groanings") are most difficult for you to bear?

5. Reread the list of sentences that begin with "Instead of…" With which statements do you most clearly identify? Why?

6. We have Jesus as our Kinsman-Redeemer, so we don't have to live like paupers. How then can we change our thinking about ourselves?

*Make Yourself at Home*

1. In your pilgrimage of learning about prayer, which posture more accurately describes you at this point: standing formally in the doorway or feeling at home on the couch? Why?

2. What are the missing prayers? What do they ask for that other prayers don't?

3. On page 162, Bob suggests a different approach to prayer. How would such an approach give us more confidence in prayer? Why do we often ignore such prayer?

4. Consider this statement: "God loves to answer His own requests." If this is true, why is it important that we think about God before talking to Him? How would this increase the need to link a life of Bible study to our prayer life?

# CHAPTER TEN

## As Big As God

1. We tend to crowd the stage of our prayers with our own needs and concerns. This leaves little room for God to receive much of our focus. Would you agree that this is "intercessory smallness"? Why or why not?

2. Bob gives the analogy of a tree that blew over because it had shallow roots. Why do we fail to think about the depth of our spiritual roots until a storm comes?

3. When have you personally experienced your roots in God as shallow? As deep?

4. Sanctuary prayer isn't simply repeatedly asking God, "Can I please know You better?" How do we explore God's character? How do we truly get to know Him better?

5. In family life and in prayer, the child who asks for that which the parent wants to give will receive a lot. Can you relate any personal experiences that illustrate this truth? Why do we so often forget this principle when it comes to prayer?

# CHAPTER ELEVEN

## Three Journeys

1. Bob discovered a previously unknown world in a gold mine. Have you ever visited another "world" that captivated you? What made it fascinating?

2. In what ways do the words "Dear heavenly Father" (or some such introduction to prayer) represent the beginning of the greatest adventure possible?

3. The journeys to hope, glory, and power are only a few journeys among many possible ones. What other prayer journeys would you like to take? How can you do so?

4. Why do believers so often see themselves as weak instead of powerful?

5. Commitments to change our prayer habits often last a few days or weeks and then run out of steam. What kind of plan could help us grow in prayer over the long haul?

# CHAPTER TWELVE

## God the Showman

1. The opening paragraphs of this chapter describe the status quo of the spirit world just before the Resurrection. How does this picture help us understand the phenomenal significance of this event?

2. Jesus told a parable of a dinner guest who was asked to vacate the seat of honor and move to a lower one. Why does embarrasment cut right to the heart of our emotions? Would you be willing to share one of your most embarrasing moments?

3. The other side of the coin is when we sit in a lower place and are invited to sit in a more honorable one. Describe the feelings that invitation would produce. Has such a thing ever happened to you?

4. Every Christian struggles against sin. Jesus Christ's name is a great power source in the fight. What are practical ways that Jesus' name and its authority really make a difference?

5. Christ's name is not a good luck charm, nor is Jesus a genie ready to pop out of a bottle and grant us our wishes. Rather, we must practice "fixing our thoughts" and "setting our hearts" on our victory in Christ. What does it mean to do these things? What disciplines, practices, or insights can we offer to help each other do them?

# CHAPTER THIRTEEN

# Tilt the Mirror

1. If we're honest, we'll admit that temptation doesn't seem to lessen as the years go by. Simplistic answers don't satisfy. Do you have any war stories of disappointment with an easy-formula approach to overcoming sin?

2. "Tilt the mirror" must not become merely another gimmick. We really share in Christ's victory. How can our position in Christ practically help us overcome temptation?

3. When it comes to the Church, are you among those who have tried it out, worn it out, or spit it out? Explain. On the positive side, what has the Church meant to you?

4. Reflect on the idea that the Church, all who believe in Christ for salvation, is favored with the privilege of being His earthly reflection. In what ways does your experience with the Church measure up? In what ways does it fail?

5. Do you agree or disagree that "we contradict ourselves when we're favorable toward Jesus and noncommittal toward His body"? Does your practice line up with your conviction? Explain.

## FIRST HYMN
### CHAPTER ONE: *Refugees Like Us*

1. Another emotional beginning is in 2 Corinthians 1:3ff, where Paul praises God for His incredible comfort.

2. The three words translated bless come from the Greek word *eulogeo*. While the NIV uses *praise* in the first instance, I've chosen *bless* in my translation to reflect the three-fold repetition of *eulogeo* which Paul used in verse 3 (cp. NASB).

3. I've drawn this fictional story from several passages: Matthew 1:1–17 (the genealogy); Psalm 90 (Moses' psalm); Exodus 33:7 (the tent of meeting); Isaiah 11:1–2 (Isaiah's prophecy of the Branch); and Luke 1:46–47 (Mary's praise).

4. The word that the NIV translates "made his dwelling" (John 1:14) comes from the Greek word *skenoo*, which we would literally translate "set a tent or tabernacle."

5. I'm indebted to Dr. Donald Sunukjian, from whom I heard this illustration.

### CHAPTER TWO: *The Rightful Owner*

1. The Hebrew word for "sanctuary" is *miqdash,* and the root, translated most often as "sanctify," is *qadash*.

2. The Greek word for "saint" is *hagios* (used in many places, not to mention Ephesians 1:1, 15) and is the same as that translated "holy" in Ephesians 1:4. "Sanctification," the process of being made holy by God, comes from the related Greek word *hagiosmos*.

### CHAPTER THREE: *The Highlight of His Day*

1. Some scholars suggest this word might be derived from baby sounds such as "abab."

2. The Greek word translated "adoption" is *huiothesia,* from *huios,* "a son," and *thesis,* "a placing."

3. Reprinted by permission of the publishers and the Loeb Classical Library from *PAPYRI, VOLUME I,* translated by A. S. Hunt and C. C. Edgar,

Cambridge, Mass.: Harvard University Press, 1932, p.31.

4. In Romans 8:16, the word "testifies" comes from the Greek word *summartureo*, "to bear witness with, confirm." It is in the present active indicative form, indicating an ongoing and current work of the Spirit in reaffirming to believers the reality of their adoption.

### *SELAH* BETHLEHEM

1. The definitions offered in the "Selah" sections are composites drawn from *Vine's Expository Dictionary of Old and New Testament Words; A Greek-English Lexicon of the Greek Language* by Arndt and Gingrich; and the *New Bible Dictionary,* 2nd edition.

### SECOND HYMN
#### *The Hidden Hope of Golgotha: Our Deliverance in the Son*

1. Also called Potter's Field (see Matthew 27:1–10).

2. 2 Kings 23:10.

3. Luke 3:22.

4. Mark 14:36.

5. "The Old Rugged Cross," by Rev. George Bennard, public domain.

### CHAPTER FOUR: *Devastation*

1. See 1 Peter 5:8 (the lion) and Hebrews 2:14–15 (fear of death). For further study, read 2 Corinthians 11:14; 1 John 3:10; and Mark 4:15.

2. Genesis 3:14.

3. Luke 13:10–17.

4. Luke 16:19–31.

5. Matthew 21:28–44.

6. Luke 13:22–30.

### CHAPTER FIVE: *But God Roars Louder*

1. These paragraphs are an adaptation of Psalm 18:7–15.

2. The Greek word for "redemption" is *apolytrosis,* built on the root word *lytron,* which means "ransom, price of release."

3. Isaiah 53.

4. This contrast between the earthly and heavenly sanctuary is beautifully described in Hebrews 9.

5. H. G. Liddell and Scott, *Abridged Greek-English Lexicon* (Oxford: Oxford University Press, 1992).

6. A. W. Tozer, *The Knowledge of the Holy,* (New York: HarperCollins Publishers Inc., 1961), 98. Used by permission

7. The Greek word is *tethrausmenous,* from *terauo.*

8. Paraphrased from *1998, 30 Days Muslim Prayer Focus,* P.O.Box 739, Buderim, Qld, 4556 Australia.

9. Many Scripture passages explain salvation, such as John 1:12; 3:16; Romans 5:8; 6:23; and Ephesians 2:8–9

## CHAPTER SIX: *It'll All Add Up Just Fine*

1. I want to thank my friend Gideon Kiongo for sharing this story with me. (Gideon wasn't the late pastor!)

2. This is the Greek word *pleroma,* often translated "fullness."

3. This is the Greek word *anakephalaioomai,* from *kephale,* which means "head."

## *SELAH* GOLGOTHA

1. I paraphrased this story from "Song of Survival" by Helen Colijn, *Reader's Digest,* November 1997, London, p.113.

## THIRD HYMN
### CHAPTER SEVEN: *Safe and Sound*

1. Greek speakers often emphasized a point by placing the pertinent words or phrases at the beginning of the sentence. Paul did that in this instance; verse 13 literally begins "In whom [Christ] you also…." Repetition is another form of emphasis. Verse 13 has two occurrences of "in whom" referring to Jesus Christ; in the Greek version of verses 1–14, there are twelve such phrases.

2. Isaiah's prophecy was figuratively sealed, keeping it from being understood (Isaiah 29:11).

3. This verb, *sphragidzo,* "to mark with a seal," is in the passive mood in this verse, meaning that the action happened to us; we did not cause it.

4. The aorist tense, which Paul used here, indicates a one-time action, normally in the past tense. In other words, we aren't bought through a *process* of being sealed. Rather, we were sealed at one point in time, at the moment we placed our individual trust in Christ for salvation.

### CHAPTER EIGHT: *Your Rustproof Inheritance*

1. "Blessed Assurance," by Fanny J. Crosby, public domain.

2. The Greek word is *arrabon;* Walter Bauer, F. Wilbur Gingrich, and Frederick W. Danker, *A Greek-English Lexicon of the New Testament and Other Early Christian Literature* (Chicago: Univ. of Chicago Press, 1979).

### PRAYER
### CHAPTER TEN: *As Big As God*

1. A. W. Tozer, *The Pursuit of God,* Christian Publications, Inc. (Harrisburg, PA, 1948). Used by permission.

2. Paul often prayed this kind of discovery prayer. Just two chapters later (Ephesians 3:14–21) his letter will erupt into another grand prayer for understanding and power.

### CHAPTER ELEVEN: *Three Journeys*

1. P. T. Forsyth, *The Soul of Prayer,* (London: Charles H. Kelly, 1916), public domain.

### DOXOLOGY
### CHAPTER TWELVE: *God the Showman*

1. "Rule" comes from the Greek word *arche,* meaning a domain or sphere of influence based on prior existence.

2. "Authority" comes from the Greek word *exousia,* meaning a freedom of choice, a right to act.

3. "Power" comes from the Greek word *dunamis,* meaning power, might, strength, force.

4. "Dominion" comes from the Greek word *kuriotes,* meaning ruling power, lordship, dominion.

5. "Title" comes from the Greek word *onoma,* meaning name, and implies rank, authority, character.

## CHAPTER THIRTEEN: *Tilt the Mirror*

1. In Ephesians 2:5, the phrase "made us alive" is *sunedzoopoiesen* (a compound of three words: "with," "alive," and "made"). In 2:6 the phrase "raised us up with" is *sunegeiren,* and "seated us with" is *sunekathisen.*

2. Romans 6 is required reading on this subject. Also, Colossians 3 makes an excellent study. In Colossians 3:5 and following, Paul tells us not to sin. Before that (verses 1–4) he tells us how to avoid sinning: by setting our minds and hearts on things above. He also explains theological basis for doing so: "Since, then, you have been raised with Christ" (verse 1), and "For you died, and your life is now hidden with Christ in God" (verse 3).